# THE LEGAL ALIEN'S
# GUIDE

# THE LEGAL ALIEN'S GUIDE

## Building a Career and Life in Chicago, Illinois

TATIANA SOROKINA

iUniverse, Inc.
New York  Lincoln  Shanghai

THE LEGAL ALIEN'S GUIDE
Building a Career and Life in Chicago, Illinois

iUniverse books may be ordered through booksellers or by contacting:

iUniverse
2021 Pine Lake Road, Suite 100
Lincoln, NE 68512
www.iuniverse.com
1-800-Authors (1-800-288-4677)

Because of the dynamic nature of the Internet, any Web addresses or links contained in this book may have changed since publication and may no longer be valid.

ISBN: 978-0-595-44622-3 (pbk)
ISBN: 978-0-595-68855-5 (cloth)
ISBN: 978-0-595-88946-4 (ebk)

Printed in the United States of America

# ACKNOWLEDGMENTS

I am very grateful to my career consultant, Kathleen Earle, from Spherion Corporation's Human Resources Consulting Group, who helped me from the very first days of my arrival in the United States. She was the first one to teach me about the value of networking and guided me during my first year in Chicago.

I am thankful to the National Association of Women Business Owners, Chicago chapter, and to the Business Network Chicago and its members for advice, enthusiasm, and opportunities for learning, personal and professional development, sharing of experiences, and networking.

I am also grateful to my family and friends for continuous support during this project, as always.

# CONTENTS

# CHAPTER 1:
# INTRODUCTION

## MY STORY

My journey to the West started when I moved from Russia to Budapest, Hungary, in 1999 to earn my MBA. After graduation in 2001, I moved to London, England, to work. So when I was looking at the prospect of moving to the United States in 2005, I really dreaded the idea of so many life-changing events in just six years. But I didn't have much of a choice. My husband was working in Chicago at the time, and one of us had to make the sacrifice.

It is popular knowledge that job changes, relocation, and marriage are three of the most stressful events in a person's life. I experienced all of them at once. My move to the United States left me feeling lonely and like an alien in the New World. My friends, family, and professional ambitions were left behind in Europe.

My husband tried to help me as much as he could, but as a medical researcher, he had no clue about the marketing/international business field in the United States. He didn't know anything about issues regarding business start-up, business development, or women in business.

So here I was standing at the crossroads, having no idea where to go or what to do next. Does this sound familiar? If you have relocated to the United States or even within the United States and are now holding this book in your hands, you probably feel just like I did a year and a half ago.

I admit I was a little lucky. When I came to Chicago, I knew one person besides my husband: Kathleen, a career consultant who was recommended to me while I was still in London. She was the first one to explain to me the importance of networking in America. According to various statistics[1], 65 to 75 percent of jobs are found through networking with people you know. That was not good news for a newcomer who didn't know anyone.

Probably the same figures are true for your own business start up and development. I meet a lot of people through various organizations I belong to. Irrespective of the nature of their business, most of them say that they get the majority of their clients through referrals.

Even if you want just to make friends in a new city, you have to know when and where to go to meet people.

I still have a piece of paper on my desk that Kathleen gave me when we first met. On the paper is a list of eight networking and support groups in the Chicago area. That's what I started with. And to be honest, I didn't start right away. It took me four months to persuade myself to get out in the world and meet total strangers. I had to force myself to approach at least one person, make an introduction, and ask for advice and help.

If you have picked up this book, you are probably experiencing the same level of stress in similar circumstances. You may feel uncomfortable with or even terrified by the idea of networking in an unfamiliar country and culture. But I learned the hard way that you will not get anywhere in America without networking.

In the beginning of my professional life, I was scared and uncomfortable at the thought of having to network. During my two-year MBA program in Budapest, I collected just a handful of business cards at the dozens of career-related events I attended. I used to stick with my classmates for the whole evening so I wouldn't have to meet any new people. After I moved to Chicago, circumstances forced me to meet hundreds of people, and I am so grateful. During the first ten events I attended in the United States, I felt awful, but things started to get better when I learned how to network. Attending a professional event is much easier when you know the answers to the following questions:

- Where you are going in your career?
- What can you expect from the event?
- What is the structure and atmosphere of the event?
- What are the advantages of attending the event?
- Who are you going to meet?

---

1    One of the sources is an article called "Importance of Networking and Relationship Building" found at http://www.esquiregroup.com/jobs_career_24.cfm

By sharing my ordeal, I hope to make your transition to American professional life much easier. I took more than a year to perform my research, analyze and filter the data, and check out various resources so that you don't have to. Traditional U.S. guidebooks sold in bookstores are travel guides that tell you how to have loads of fun on vacation or books on history, culture, and traditions. When you relocate somewhere *to live*, theaters and restaurants are the last things you worry about. You want to find a job (or start your own business) and find colleagues, customers, and friends—people who share your professional and social interests.

This guide is the best help you will ever get. I have carefully selected and classified organizations, clubs, and networking groups into categories according to a person's needs and interests. Every entry comes with a short description of the organization's mission or purpose, advantages, event structure, and extra services.

This guide is useful for people who relocate not only to Chicago but to any U.S. city. Two-thirds of the organizations I describe have chapters around the country.

Furthermore, this guide will be extremely useful to Americans, too. If you have lived all your life, say, in Denver or New York City, you may feel just as lost in Chicago as a legal alien. You will definitely benefit from the help of the local resources that I have compiled in this book. I have a colleague who relocated from the Chicago suburbs to downtown Chicago, and she was shocked to find out that life in the city is *very* different from life in the suburbs. She felt lonely and lost for several months while she struggled to find her place in the city and rebuild her network.

Usually, as the saying goes, nothing worth having in life ever comes easy, but since I have already "invented the bicycle," I will let you use it. Enjoy the ride!

# SYMBOLS

In my guide, I use several symbols. Here is the legend to assist your reading:

*—I personally attended a meeting or meetings of this group.
Ch—Chicago
IL—Illinois
N—Nationwide
$—fee applies (for events and/or membership)
FREE—free events and/or membership

# CHAPTER 2:
## CHURCHES

When I first arrived in Chicago, my career advisor, Kathleen, introduced me to the concept of networking and told me that church communities are the best place to start, especially for people who are not very outgoing or have never really networked before. She was right. I never felt awkward, unwelcome, or out of place in any of the church meetings I attended, even though I didn't belong to the congregation or to any religious denomination widely spread in United States.[2]

**Good for:** career transition, some business development, getting to know your local community

**Advantages:** In the United States, nearly every Christian church (I cannot speak about other confessions since I am speaking only from personal experience) has an active community. Whether you live in a big city or a small town, there will be a church nearby. I strongly recommend that you start your journey at your local church.

Every week, churches organize various events, which often include educational programs for kids and networking opportunities for adults in transition. The latter are particularly good. They are free, and you can go to a couple of meetings and decide if you want to become more involved. People in a church are always very nice and sincerely trying to help each other. After all, this is God's house, and he taught us this way.

You don't need to be Christian to attend these meetings, and no one will force you to come for worship. I attended only networking meetings, and we had a couple of Hindu and Chinese attendees. As an additional benefit, though

---

2    I am a Russian Orthodox, which means I am Christian, but my church is different from more common Catholic, Protestant, or Lutheran churches in America.

the majority of other associations, clubs, and organizations close for the summer, church communities carry on with their events all year round.

**Structure:** Networking meetings are usually held once a week or once every two weeks and last one to two hours. The size of the group varies depending on the size of the local community. I have been to meetings with five people and to meetings with up to fifty people. A guest speaker opens the meeting with a presentation on a topic of general interest usually related to career transition, psychology, or networking. Attendees are always given feedback forms where they can suggest topics for future presentations. The opening presentation is followed by a networking session, either informal or structured.[3] That's when you introduce yourself to other people, get to know them, and tell them what you are looking for. Don't forget a pen and a notebook. People will be pouring ideas into you. It is worthwhile to distribute your resumes, handbills, or business cards[4] to participants. They will contact you if they hear of something that might interest you. People here are very helpful and truly believe that what goes around comes around.

**Extras:** In addition to networking, you will get many free handouts with useful articles and other resources at every meeting. In between meetings, the group will send out e-mail newsletters with information on other groups' meetings, job leads, and educational seminars, most of which are also free of charge.

Here are some church communities that organize great networking events in Chicagoland:

**\*St. Hubert's Job and Networking Support Ministry** (FREE, IL)
*http://finance.groups.yahoo.com/group/St_Hubert_Job_Ministry/*
This is a fellowship of men and women with a common desire to become employed or seek career advancement through a Christian forum. There are no dues or fees for membership. The group supports itself through voluntary

---

3     Structured networking consists of ten to fifteen people placed around a table. (There are several tables organized at the same time.) Everyone gives a two- to three-minute speech about himself/herself and asks for whatever help he/she needs. The other people around the table give advice, leads, etc. In some organizations, this networking happens at lunch or dinner, and people change tables every course (you are assigned to a certain table each time) so that you can talk to the maximum amount of people. With informal networking, everyone is gathered in one big room, and you can walk around and talk to whomever you want.

4     This is also true of any other event you plan to attend. You should have at least your business cards with you. Even if you are not working yet, you can make your own cards with your name, contact information, and a brief personal statement.

contributions. Meetings take place once every two weeks in Hoffman Estates, and they always include a structured networking session. There are usually fifty to sixty attendees at every meeting. Total membership as of November 2006 is 484.

*Saint Chrysostom's Employment Council (FREE, Ch)

This is a smaller, more intimate group (usually ten to fifteen people attend) that meets in downtown Chicago every week. The networking is informal. Every person is asked to speak about his or her news or progress since the last meeting. This group will be like a steering committee motivating you to achieve your goals.

More church job support groups can be found at *http://www.workministry. com/job_support_groups.shtml*. The Web site gives information on work ministries in twenty-five states and Washington DC.

# CHAPTER 3:
# COUNTRY-SPECIFIC
# GROUPS

**Good for:** career transition, business development, cultural activities, getting acquainted with fellow countrymen

**Advantages:** Every major U.S. city has a number of chambers of commerce from different countries. Though the main goal of these chambers is to facilitate economic exchanges between their country's companies and American companies, they organize various business, cultural, political, or networking events on a regular basis (several per week). A chamber of commerce is a great place to meet your fellow countrymen, people who have been living in the United States for some time. They have already gone through what you are going through and can help you with orientation. This is your little "home away from home." It is a great place to develop your business whether you are working for someone or an entrepreneur.

**Structure:** This depends on the event, which might be a cocktail party, a conference, a seminar, a breakfast/lunch meeting, or something else. The turnout is usually very good, ranging from fifty to several hundred people.

**Extras:** You will receive free newsletters with all sorts of useful information, including job leads. Some chambers organize educational seminars on various topics ranging from immigration to cultural exchange.

Here are the major national chambers in Chicago:

America-Israel Chamber of Commerce Chicago ($)
*http://www.americaisrael.org*

British American Business Council ($)
*http://www.babcc.org/*

CzechTrade ($)
*http://www.czechtradeoffices.com/Global*

*French American Chamber of Commerce ($)
*http://www.facc-chicago.com/index.htm*

I would like to draw your attention to FACC because of its exciting schedule of events, especially social ones. From Mardi Gras Masquerade to wine tasting to Passport to France soiree, every month FACC has something special to offer. In addition, FACC will send e-mail advertising other interesting social events in Chicago even if they are not organized by FACC. Some of these events charge a fee and others, like the fashion show and cocktail party for ladies recently organized by Escada, are free.

To receive these e-mail announcements, you don't need to be an FACC member; you just need to attend one of their events. Drop your business card into their "cards bowl," and they will add you to their distribution list.

German American Chamber of Commerce
*http://www.gaccom.org*

Italian American Chamber of Commerce
*http://www.italianchamber.us*

Polish American Chamber of Commerce
*http://www.pacc.polaccess.com*

Puerto Rican Chamber of Commerce of Illinois
*http://www.prcci.com*

Swedish American Chamber of Commerce of Chicago
*http://www.sacc-usa.org/chicago*

Also present in Illinois are the Cuban, Guatemalan, Japanese, Korean, and Philippine chambers of commerce, but, as of November 2006, they don't have Web sites. Addresses and phone numbers are listed in the yellow pages.

# LANGUAGE-BASED GROUPS

Language-based groups unite people, but not necessarily people of one nationality (for example, Spanish-speakers come from many countries). People who don't want to lose fluency in a native or second language, who are interested in the culture of a region, or who just want to make friends come together in these groups.

**Good for:** making friends, furthering education, some business development
**Advantages:** Groups are very informal and meet in nice locations. One can brush up on foreign languages.
**Structure:** cocktail-party style, informal networking, guest-speaker presentations, attendance of twenty to forty people

*Grouppe Professionel Francophone ($, Ch)
*http://www.gpfchicago.org*
   The main goal of the group (as stated on its Web site) is "to unite nice people from various countries who would like to discuss diverse topics in French." The monthly meetings are actually cocktail parties with one or two guest speakers and pleasant discussions. I love to attend this great group because I love France and speak French.

*Chicago Council on Global Affairs (membership FREE, events $, IL)
*http://www.globalchicago.org*
   I will talk in detail about this organization in Chapter 4 but regarding language groups, I need to mention that the Chicago Council on Global Affairs organizes foreign-language dinners for members who are "interested in conversing about global affairs in their native language or a learned tongue. These small, intimate dinners take place regularly at restaurants, usually in downtown Chicago. Dinners are open to all Council members. While no registration fee is charged, participants do pay for their own dinners."[5]
   As of December 2006, the council holds monthly dinners in the following languages: Arabic, Bulgarian, Chinese, German, Greek, French, Italian, Polish, Russian, and Spanish.

---

5   The information is from the Council's Web site

# CULTURAL AND HERITAGE CENTERS

Usually located in the major cities, they may not be numerous but are worth checking out. Larger cities with more immigrants will have more cultural centers.

**Good for:** cultural and educational events, meeting fellow countrymen

**Advantages:** membership gives access to associated libraries and museums. You will receive free newsletters and may be able to use the center's facilities for meetings.

**Structure:** varies depending on the event

Here is a selection of cultural/heritage centers in Chicago:

**Irish American Heritage Center** ($, Ch)
*http://www.irishamhc.com*

**Bulgarian American Association** ($, Ch)
*http://baachicago.com/default.aspx*
The Bulgarian community is quite active in Chicago.

Chicago also has Latvian and Bulgarian cultural centers, but they don't have Web sites as of November 2006. Their addresses and phone numbers can be found through a Google search.

# CHAPTER 4:
# INTERNATIONAL
# ORGANIZATIONS

International organizations are usually located in major cities. They usually have large, active memberships. They offer nearly all possible types of activities from political to business to cultural.

**Good for:** There is usually something for everyone because the organizations are big and their activities are varied.

**Advantages:** You have an opportunity to meet many internationals like yourself, which helps you to overcome the feeling of being foreign or alien. You can share experiences and get advice. The large membership offers many opportunities for outreach. For example, you might advertise your business on the organization's newsletter or Web site. Organizations are usually active not only in the major cities but statewide. This is ideal if you are looking for a job or trying to develop your own business on an international arena.

**Structure:** varies depending on the event

**\*World Trade Centers** ($, N)
*http://www.wtcc.org* (Chicago link)
*http://world.wtca.org/portal/site/wtcaonline* (global page)
There are more than forty world trade centers across the United States. Sometimes, a world trade center is more of a real-estate organization (as it was in NY). World Trade Center Chicago is more of an international trade and international relations development organization.

World Trade Center Chicago programs include the following:

- Business matchmaking (inbound and outbound trade delegations)
- Trade and investment programs
- Research
- Educational programs
- Roundtable discussions

### *Organization of Women in International Trade ($, N)
*http://www.owit.org*
*http://www.owitchicago.org* (Chicago link)

This is a nonprofit professional organization committed to fostering the advancement of women in international trade by providing networking and educational opportunities to enhance their knowledge of global trade issues.

The members are diverse and include both men and women who share an interest in all facets of international trade. Members are professionals from many industries and business sectors including banking and finance, communications, customs and trade law, education, government and diplomacy, import/export, insurance, technology, nonprofit organizations, transportation, and other trade-related services.

It's a great forum, especially for women. You can meet a lot of bright, interesting, successful women who will be very glad to share with you their international experiences and the lessons they've learned, as well as give you advice and guidance.

The events are usually scheduled once a month and have two parts: (1) a presentation from a distinguished speaker (or panel of speakers) working in an international field and (2) informal networking over drinks.

### *International Trade Club of Chicago ($, IL)
*http://www.itcc.org*

As mentioned on the ITCC Web site, this organization has several aims:

- Foster and expand international trade and investment
- Encourage the profession of international business management on a high ethical plane
- Furnish its members with a medium for exchange of experience and a forum for the discussion of problems of mutual interest

- Seek by concerted action to remove barriers and obstacles that may interfere with the development of international trade and investment

- Promote better understanding and appreciation of the significance of international trade and investment

This organization stands out by providing regular "speaker and networking" meetings as well as many educational programs. Examples include the following:

- Professional development programs and symposia

- Seminars, technical presentations, and topical meetings

- Sector-focused working groups (e.g., manufacturing committee, nanotechnology committee, etc.)

**\*The Chicago Council on Global Affairs** (membership FREE, events $, IL) *http://www.globalchicago.org*

On its Web site, the council shares its mission:

"… [to] enhance Chicago's strengths as a global city and raise awareness—both here and abroad—of Chicago's global connections. It acts as a catalyst to bring Chicago's diverse global resources closer together and spread information on the city's many global connections. It does this by:

- identifying Chicago's global assets and its economic, social, intellectual, and cultural links to the rest of the world;

- facilitating communication and collaboration among internationally minded groups;

- helping Chicagoans understand the challenges and opportunities of globalization."

The great thing about this organization is that membership is free, which means you can list your company in its "global resources" directory and advertise events on its monthly calendar at no cost. This calendar is a fantastic resource in itself. Many organizations (business, cultural, political, and educational) list their events here. There are up to ten different events scheduled on any given day, and you can choose the ones you want to attend, and learn more about the organizations that arrange them.

*Eurocircle (membership FREE, events $, N)
*http://www.eurocircle.com*
"EuroCircle is an informal community for European professionals and Europhiles—married or single—with over 45,000 members. With no political, religious, or ethnic affiliations, Eurocircle.com is a place where you can exchange ideas, tips, professional contacts, make friends, and more. You can meet people offline at local events, online through the membership features, or via the forums."[6]

This is more of a social club. It's fantastic for making friends in a new place, and people are always friendly. In Chicago, Eurocircle organizes monthly gatherings over cocktails and large parties on major holidays such as Halloween, St. Valentine's Day, etc. These events are not just for Europeans, and I always see people from Latin America, India, and elsewhere. Everyone is welcome!

Eurocircle is now active in Atlanta, Boston, Chicago, Dallas, Denver, Los Angeles, Miami, New York, Orange County, Philadelphia, San Diego, San Francisco, and Washington DC.

Eurocircle offers several circles in one city depending on people's interests. For instance, in New York City, there are dance, tennis, VIP, and FrancoFolie subcircles. You can suggest your own subcircle and organize your own events, or you can form a full circle if there is none where you live.

*International Business Professionals Group (membership FREE, events $, IL)
*http://finance.groups.yahoo.com/group/International_Business_Professional*
This is an informal group of professionals whose careers are connected to international business or who are interested in pursuing careers in this field.

It is "a not-for-profit organization and community; providing knowledge, skills and resources through Chicago/Midwest-based members with significant international experience." Their mission is:
- "to act as a members forum for the exchange of information and knowledge about international business;
- To market their members knowledge, experience and skills either for the purpose of gaining permanent employment or provide professional services to companies, foreign and domestic trade/business development organizations and industry associations."[7]

---

6    The information is from EuroCircle Web site
7    The information is from IBPG Web site

The group meets once every three weeks, and the meetings include formal educational presentations, discussions and roundtables, and informal networking.

### International Visitors Center Chicago ($, Ch)
*http://www.ivcc.org*

Traditional visitors centers can be found in nearly every city in the United States. They aim to provide tourism-related information. International visitor centers, like the one in Chicago, have a different mission. IVCC works with foreign delegations "to provide opportunities for face-to-face professional and social interaction between visitors and their American counterparts that enable a better understanding of each other's way of life and that promote Chicago as an important international center for culture, commerce, and tourism."[8]

**Good for:** getting to know people from different cultures, making friends, interacting socially, improving language skills

**Advantages:** You can meet with delegations from various countries and learn about internship and volunteer opportunities (including work as an interpreter). You can participate in receptions, forums, and leadership programs.

### International Association of Business Communicators ($, N)
*http://www.iabc.com*
*http://www.iabcchicago.com* (Chicago chapter)

IABC is a global network that provides "the content, the credibility, and the community to help communication professionals succeed in their careers." There are IABC chapters worldwide, with more than sixty in the United States. Chicago's chapter proclaims its mission to "provide services, activities, and networking opportunities to help people achieve professional excellence and drive the success of their organizations through effective communication strategies and practices."[9]

This organization unites professionals working in the following fields: public relations, employee communications, community relations, graphic design, marketing, media production, and printing.

**Good for:** professional and business development, networking

**Advantages:** IABC organizes plenty of events for communications professionals, including seminars, forums presentations, and business development lunches. Most of these events include an informal-networking section. These events are great for learning and meeting professionals in your field and building relationships. The Chicago

---

8   The information is from IVCC Web site

9   The information is from IABC Web site

chapter claims to organize around twenty-two events per year from September to June.

**Structure:** varies depending on the event, but there is usually a formal presentation and informal networking session included

**Extras:** IABC organizes an annual awards event to recognize outstanding work of local communicators.

# CHAPTER 5:
# LOCAL ORGANIZATIONS

Every town in the United States has a local chamber of commerce. There is typically a membership fee ($), but events are often free for members. The bigger the city, the more local chambers it has. There is usually one for each district or community. Chicago has more than thirty local chambers, which are listed later in this chapter.

The main objective of a local chamber is to be an organization for local businesses that supports and encourages community and economic development.

**Good for:** getting to know your local community and what's happening in your neighborhood, helping your business develop, and searching for jobs.

**Advantages:** These are small communities that focus on issues important to your neighborhood. They organize business and social events, sponsor promotions, and help small businesses in their areas with various day-to-day issues such as advertising. Some of the chambers give discounts to members if members shop for products and services in their neighborhoods.

In Chicago, the local chambers are also famous for organizing street festivals—each a unique Chicago experience.

**\*Chicagoland Chamber of Commerce**
*http://www.chicagolandchamber.org/home.asp*
This chamber represents a "unified business voice of greater Chicago [Chicago and its suburbs] representing business interests at the city, county, regional and state levels." This specific chamber organizes a lot of educational events, seminars, conferences, and roundtables. It has programs for entrepreneurs and businesses planning to expand internationally.

This chamber also gives you an opportunity to come to some free events before you decide if this is the organization for you and pay membership dues.

These free events include monthly business development breakfasts, where you can meet new and prospective members, learn about the chamber, and network.

Local chambers in Chicago are:

Albany Park Chamber of Commerce
*http://www.albanyparkchamber.org*

Belmont-Central Chamber of Commerce
*http://www.belmontcentral.org*

Chicago Chinatown Chamber of Commerce
*http://www.chicagochinatown.org*

Chicago Southland Chamber of Commerce
*http://www.chicagosouthland.com*

Edgewater Chamber of Commerce
*http://www.edgewater.org*

Edison Park Chamber of Commerce
*http://www.edisonpark.com*

Hyde Park Chamber of Commerce
*http://www.hpchamber.com*

Jefferson Park Chamber of Commerce
*http://www.jeffersonpark.net*

Lakeview Chamber of Commerce
*http://www.lakeviewchamber.com*

*Lakeview East Chamber of Commerce
*http://www.lakevieweast.com*

*Lincoln Park Chamber of Commerce
*http://www.lincolnparkchamber.com*

Lincoln Square Chamber of Commerce
*http://www.lincolnsquare.org*

Little Village Chamber of Commerce
*http://www.LaVillitaChamber.com*

Northcenter Chamber of Commerce
*http://www.northcenterchamber.com*

Norwood Park Chamber of Commerce
*http://www.norwoodpark.org*

Ravenswood Chamber of Commerce
*http://www.ravenswoodchamber.com*

Roscoe Village Chamber of Commerce
*http://www.roscoe-village.org*

Streeterville Chamber of Commerce
*http://www.streetervillechamber.org*

West Ridge Chamber of Commerce
*http://www.westridgechamber.org*

West Town Chamber of Commerce
*http://www.westtownchamber.org*

Wicker Park and Bucktown Chamber of Commerce
*http://www.wickerparkbucktown.com*

Other Chicago-area chambers listed in the yellow pages but without a Web site as of November 2006 include: Beverly Area CC, Cermak Road CC, Fulleron Avenue CC, East Side CC, Edgebrook CC, Garfield Park CC, Madison & Western CC, McCormick CC, Montrose Kedzie CC, Pilsen Together CC, and South Chicago CC.

# CHAPTER 6:
## MINORITY
## ORGANIZATIONS

This chapter addresses services specific to gender, ethnicity, and sexual orientation, but I have devoted the biggest part of the chapter to women's organizations for the following reasons:

1.  I based this book on my personal experiences. As a woman, I naturally investigated a lot of organizations for women. It would be a shame not to pass this knowledge to my readers.
2.  When a family has to relocate, it is often because the husband has landed a job in a new place. This makes the adjustment easier for the man, who will have a circle of his work colleagues to network and make friends with while his wife will be more or less on her own.
3.  There are not many "men only" organizations to speak of. Those that exist are described later in this chapter.

## WOMEN'S ORGANIZATIONS

The United States is a great country in which to be a woman. It has an enormous number of organizations, clubs, and associations that devote all their time and attention to the support and development of women looking for educational opportunities, social interaction, and professional development. There are also services for women who would like to start their own businesses. Some organizations are local; others are active nationwide. But they all have one thing in common: they always make you feel welcome, try to help you with anything you need, and strive to motivate and encourage you. Women-owned businesses flourish in USA. Many women's organizations were of great help to me, and I am thankful to all of them for all the support.

**\*NAWBO (National Association of Women Business Owners)** (membership $, events FREE and $, N)
*http://www.nawbo.org*
*http://www.nawbochicago.org* (Chicago chapter)

According to its Web site:

National Association of Women Business Owners propels women entrepreneurs into economic, social, and political spheres of power worldwide. Members have access to a variety of services that will help their business to achieve greater visibility, credibility, and profitability.

NAWBO is an organization, which works to:

STRENGTHEN the wealth-creating capacity of our members and promote economic development

CREATE innovative and effective changes in the business culture

BUILD strategic alliances, coalitions, and affiliations

TRANSFORM public policy and influence opinion.

NAWBO is present in virtually every metropolitan area in the United States. Each state is represented by several chapters, and there are three chapters in Illinois. Though a national organization, it is affiliated with international organizations including the World Association of Women Entrepreneurs (FCEM), the International Alliance for Women, and Global Summit of Women to promote women's entrepreneurship.

You don't need to be a business owner to become a member and benefit from what NAWBO has to offer. If you work for someone else, you can be a corporate member. The issues that NAWBO addresses are relevant to all women irrespective of their occupation or profession.

**Good for:** developing your business, making friends, finding educational opportunities. You don't have to be a business owner to join, and you don't need to work in the field of business or management. In the Chicago chapter, I met everyone from lawyers to reflexology therapists to a flute player.

**Advantages:** This organization tries to build long-term relationships between the women it unites. These relationships are based on trust, support, and a sincere desire to help each other. It is not uncommon for NAWBO members to buy a lot of products or services from their fellow NAWBO members, thus helping each other's businesses to grow.

**Structure:** NAWBO organizes different types of events from networking dinners to roundtables to conferences.

**Extras:** Members have access to various free events and services that most other organizations do not provide. These include the following:

- Committees—you may sit on a committee of your interest (diversity, membership, awards, etc.).
- Roundtables and interest groups—there are numerous roundtables that serve various needs. In Chicago, these groups include the under-35 roundtable, Creatives SIG, African American Latino Asian (ALA) roundtable, Windy City Investors, etc.
- Leads groups—there are seven in Chicago as of November 2006. Every member can start one in her own neighborhood. The goal of the leads groups is to have one professional from a certain industry (say, one marketing consultant, one coach, one real estate agent, etc.) and build relationships between members in the group. Members help each other find leads for each other's businesses.

The advantage of these groups is that meetings are free. You can participate in as many groups as you want,[10] develop close ties and friendships, and help each other to grow.

Other free opportunities include the following:

- Speaking opportunities to help you gain visibility
- Help from the advisory board, which will spend up to two hours analyzing your business and then recommend improvements to what you are doing
- Opportunities to win awards and gain visibility
- NAWBO Neighborhood Networking, which allows you to visit informal networking events in various neighborhoods, meet with people, learn about local businesses, and promote what you do

---

10   You can participate in several committees and roundtables but belong only to one leads group.

In addition, organizations and companies supporting NAWBO (such as UPS) provide discounts to NAWBO members for their products and services.

NAWBO allows you to come to free events known as Connecting Points events (held once a quarter) before you become a member. At these events, you can meet new and prospective members, network, and learn how NAWBO and NAWBO Neighborhood Networking operate.

### American Business Women's Association ($, N)

*http://www.abwahq.org*
*http://www.abwa-chicago.org* (Chicago Chapter)

While NAWBO directs its efforts toward supporting women entrepreneurs, AWBA aims to help a wider audience of businesswomen whether they work in small, privately owned companies or in big corporations.

The mission of AWBA is to bring together businesswomen of diverse occupations and to provide opportunities for women to help themselves and others grow personally and professionally through leadership, education, networking support, and national recognition. AWBA operates in nearly every state in the country.

**Good for:** professional development, education, career transition, connecting with people

**Advantages:** AWBA members can participate in its various professional-development training programs, which include leadership development programs, MBA Essentials, Management Certificate Series, and in-depth business skills training. AWBA members can get tuition reimbursement for approved, accredited classes.

AWBA also provides networking opportunities in local chapters on a monthly basis as well as organizes national conferences.

Recognition is an important advantage, too. Each year, in addition to national awards and recognition ceremonies, local chapters and networks honor members who make significant accomplishments in education, leadership, and professional and civic activities.

**Structure:** varies depending on the event

**Extras:** AWBA members receive a free bimonthly national magazine, *Women in Business*. Members also receive benefits from national corporate sponsors that support ABWA; these companies offer discounts on their products and services.

**Women's Business Development Center** ($, Ch)
*http://www.wbdc.org*

"The Women's Business Development Center (WBDC) is a nationally and internationally recognized not-for-profit organization established to work with women to launch new businesses and strengthen existing businesses in the Chicago area."[11]

**Good for:** starting or developing your own business, educational purposes, meeting other likeminded women, and making friends

**Advantages:** "WBDC services are available in Spanish and English, and include business assessments, loan packaging, public and private sector procurement assistance, classes/workshops, and individualized counseling on all aspects of business development, management, and strategy. The WBDC also provides assistance to develop home- and center-based child care businesses. In addition, the WBDC offers a nationally recognized certification for Women Business Enterprises (WBEs) and is active in advocacy issues related to women-owned businesses on the local, state, and federal levels."[12]

**Structure:** varies depending on the event; events include conferences, seminars, brown-bag lunches, etc.

**\*Chicago Women's Network** (membership FREE, events $, Ch)
*http://www.cw-network.org/aboutus.asp*

Chicago Women's Network is a new organization that emerged after the collapse of ChicWIT organization in April 2007. CW-Network picked up most of ChicWIT's functions and members.

CW-Network offers a way "to connect with a supportive and diverse community of professional women representing all areas of business and levels of experience and expertise." It gives an opportunity to "share resources, expertise, and experience, and form life-long strategic alliances, friendships, and business relationships."

**Good for:** networking, making connections and friends, job search and developing your business.

**Advantages:** CW-Network organizes monthly networking events starting from June 2007 which are similar to networking events organized by other organizations. What makes CW-Network stand out is free of charge online moderated email discussions. When you sign up to the network you will receive daily e-mail digests with various discussion topics. You can share your expertise and give other people advice or ask for advice yourself. You can ask for help in vir-

---

11   The information is from WBDC Web site
12   The information is from WBDC Web site

tually *any* field, for instance: if you are looking for a job or a good nanny or a plumber, if you are selling a dinner table or looking to buy a used car. I personally found a great dentist with the help of this network.

### *Professional Women's Club of Chicago ($, Ch)

*http://www.pwcc.org*

"In PWCC, women are connecting with women for growth and development; it gives them an opportunity to broaden their professional, personal, and business contacts."[13]

**Good for:** networking, making connections and friends, starting a job search, developing your business

**Advantages:** PWCC is a "community of successful professional women, which represents a variety of business backgrounds and levels of experience. The diversity of the members means that you'll meet people from organizations very different from your own. At PWCC events, you're likely to encounter women in banking, technology, accounting, law, finance, hospitality, real estate, communications, human resources, executive search, career coaching, fashion and design, and a host of other fields. Whether they work for large corporations or run their own businesses, PWCC members are entrepreneurial, resourceful, and bubbling over with fresh ideas that you can use."[14]

**Structure:** Networking lunches (sometimes structured, sometimes informal) usually take place once a month. On average, there are sixty to eighty attendees. The lunch consists of a networking session and a presentation usually given by a famous, distinguished woman who shares her pearls of wisdom with regard to her industry. She may speak about her position and how she got there and share tips on how to be successful and achieve your personal and professional dreams. You can attend two events per year without becoming a member.

**Extras:** At a couple of lunches during the year, there will be no presentation, just networking. One of these lunches is named "What's your request?" At this lunch, women sit at separate tables (with fifteen to twenty people per table), and each woman is given three to five minutes to give an "elevator" speech and make requests for help. These requests can be related to her personal or professional life, and other women around the table will give advice.

---

13   The information is from PWCC Web site
14   The information is from PWCC Web site

### Empowering[15] Women Network ($, IL)

*http://www.empoweringwomen.net*

EWN is a professional women's organization "focused on leadership and the advancement of professional women. [It is] a full service women's organization offering its members and guests, monthly networking events, business-related roundtables, business development training, business coaching and mentoring, all guided by the belief that truly successful women nurture their health and well-being, relationships and personal growth as well as their careers."[16]

**Good for:** networking, making connections and friends, developing your business

**Advantages:** Networking events take place once a month in a different suburban town in the Chicago area. It is easier for working mothers to come to these events in their neighborhood rather than to commute to downtown Chicago, where most of the other events are organized.

**Structure:** monthly meetings with a networking session and a presentation on an issue related to empowering women

### Network for Empowering Women (membership $, events FREE, N)

*http://www.newentrepreneurs.com*

The mission of the network is "to create a global community for women entrepreneurs to experience business, personal, financial, and spiritual fulfillment through connections with other likeminded women."[17]

**Good for:** networking, making connections and friends, developing business

**Advantages:** This network organizes monthly face-to-face meetings in several locations in California and in Boston, MA (not in Chicago yet), but it does hold a virtual monthly meeting by telephone for all members nationwide. As mentioned on the network's Web site: "Each meeting shares many of the features of the local meetings, including round-robin introductions for attendees, acknowledgements, announcements, and inspirational closing 'circle' meditation." Each meeting features a different "on-call expert" presenting a topic chosen for its tangible, immediately applicable value to women entrepreneurs. Experts present for approximately twenty minutes, and a question-and-answer period with callers follows.

---

15  Tip: if you Google the phrase "empowering women" in your local area, you will find a lot of women's clubs, associations, networks, etc. I have included some examples of organizations with these key words in their titles. Apparently, it is a popular trend in America nowadays.

16  The information is from EWN Web site

17  The information is from Network for Empowering Women Web site

**Extras:** The network promotes a number of educational audio programs dedicated to various issues of small-business development. These can be bought on CD from the network's Web site.

## EWomenNetwork.com ($, N)
*http://www.ewomennetwork.com*

EWomenNetwork.com is a big organization operating in most US states and in Canada. Its goal is "to help female business owners and professionals achieve their goals. They want to support women's growth by purchasing their products and services, provide them access to needed resources, and connect them with others who share their passion for achievement and prosperity."[18]

**Good for:** business development and making connections, whether you are a business owner or employed by a company

**Advantages:** This is purely a networking forum that gets together once a month over lunch to network and promote your business.

**Structure:** This is usually a one and a half to two-hour luncheon that begins with thirty minutes of informal networking followed by an "accelerated networking lunch." During this luncheon, women can:

- promote who they are and what they do;
- ask for what they specifically need from others;
- develop new business alliances and friends;
- and learn new ideas and strategies for promoting their businesses and generating more revenue.

At certain lunches, women can showcase and sell their products on display tables.

**Extras:** Every member gets her own page on eWomenNetwork.com where she can promote herself, her company, her products and services, etc.

## Network of Women Entrepreneurs (Ch, $)
*http://www.nwe-chicago.com*

NWE is an organization "where women business owners can get support and encouragement from others in their same circumstances."[19] The main goals of the network are to encourage community among women; to promote the exchange of business within the group; and to educate, facilitate, and support women's growth in all aspects of their lives.

---

18　The information is from EWomenNetwork Web site

19　This information is from NWE Web site

**Good for:** networking, professional development, business development
**Advantages:** The policy of NWE is to limit membership to one person per industry or business type. This "affords NWE members the ability to speak freely about business and share ideas, solutions, and suggestions with one another. This also keeps the group more intimate, providing members the opportunity to really know one another."[20] The network organizes various events that are educational (such as seminars) and entertaining as well as members-only monthly meetings where women can get referrals and ask for advice.
**Structure:** varies depending on the event

### Step Up Women's Network (N, $)
*http://www.stepupwomensnetwork.org/index.php*
Step Up Women's Network is a nonprofit organization "dedicated to strengthening community resources for women and girls. Through hands-on community service, mentoring, and fundraising for women's health and critical issues, we educate and activate our membership to ensure that women and girls have the tools they need to create a better future."[21] This organization has active chapters in Chicago, New York, and Los Angeles.
**Good for:** networking, professional development, social interaction
**Advantages:** this organization offers a very wide range of activities. A woman can volunteer through the diverse community programs, advance her career or grow her business by taking advantage of various professional development and mentorship programs, support women's health issues, or participate in dynamic social-networking opportunities.
**Structure:** varies depending on the event

### The Links Inc (N, $)
*http://www.linksinc.org*
The Links is a not-for-profit organization of more than ten thousand women of color committed "to enhancing the quality of life in our communities"[22]— through civic, educational, and cultural aims. The organization's commitment to community service is realized through four main facets: national trends and services, services to youth, international trends and services and the arts. The organization is active in forty-two states, and there are usually several chapters per state.
**Good for:** social, educational, and personal development

---

20   This information is from NEW Web site
21   The information is from Step Up Web site
22   The information is from The Links Web site

**Advantages:** This is a very active organization. It organizes many events including conferences, summits, workshops, luncheons, and parties. The Links stresses educational and wellness issues and supports various charitable causes. This is a good organization if you would like to become active in the community and be involved in the issues relevant to women of color in the United States and internationally.

**Structure:** varies depending on the event

**Extras:** once a quarter, each area of the organization (there are 4 areas that unite several states and chapters) publishes a comprehensive newsletter about all regional activities and achievements. Chicago is part of the central area, whose fall 2006 newsletter had forty-four pages.

## Direct Selling Women's Alliance ($, N)

*http://www.mydswa.org*

DSWA is a nationwide organization that provides education, networking, and support to women with a network-marketing, party-plan, or home-based business. This is an online and offline community. Though a lot of activity happens on the Web site, DSWA has local chapters (bigger, formalized gatherings) and "Success Circles" (smaller, informal meetings) in at least twenty-three states (not in Illinois, though) and Canada that meet on a regular basis. Women in Illinois can join the online community.

**Good for:** direct marketing, business development, career change

**Advantages:** All members can create a page on the DSWA Web site where they can promote their products, and place ads to recruit people in their network marketing teams. In addition, members can participate in live training sessions or can listen to archived sessions related to direct selling.

**Extras:** On its Web site, DSWA sells a lot of educational literature related to direct selling and network marketing.

## National Association of Baby Boomer Women ($, N)

*http://www.nabbw.com*

This is a nationwide organization whose goal is to "empower women to explore life and live their passions." Chicago-area women can join this predominantly online networking community.

**Good for:** connecting with people, making friends, starting or developing a business

**Advantages:** this unique organization offers many free services to its members. Some of these services include:

- Financial and legal advice
- Promotion of a member's business or Web site on the NABBW site
- Midlife coaching,
- Advice on publishing a book
- Teleconferences related to boomer-women issues
- Access to its online forum

**Extras:** Numerous extras include a choice of free publications and discounts on certain products and services.

### Federation of Women Contractors ($, Ch)
*http://www.fwcchicago.com/welcome.htm*
    The mission of FWC is to promote advancement of entrepreneurial women in the construction industry.
**Good for:** job search or business development in the construction industry
**Advantages:** FWC distributes 2,500 copies of its membership directory to majority contractors, property owners, and federal, state, and local government agencies. FWC organizes various industry-related seminars, legislative lobbying, and monthly networking meetings.

### Women Helping Empower Women (WHEW) (events $, Ch)
*http://whewchicago.org/default.aspx*
    This is a new nonprofit organization that emerged in October 2006. It proclaims its goal as "enhancing women's lives through educational, social, and business professional networking opportunities. WHEW also serves to fundraise on behalf of creditable nonprofit organizations committed to helping the lives of women."[23]
    Though it had only one networking event in October 2006, it's worth checking out from time to time because of its unique devotion to raising money for organizations helping women. The aforesaid event was to support charities helping victims of breast cancer and domestic violence. This humanitarian organization is destined to grow in the future and to offer great social and business networking opportunities.

---

23   The information is from WHEW Web site

**Black Women Lawyers' Association** ($, Ch)
*http://www.bwla.org*
The mission of BWLA is to "identify and address issues and concerns unique to African American women lawyers and judges; to improve the administration of justice by increasing the participation of African American women and other minorities throughout the legal system and to advance civil and human rights."[24]
**Good for:** business development, networking, and sharing and gaining knowledge and expertise
**Advantages:** BWLA has regular roundtable meetings where important issues for this minority group are addressed. The discussion is led by a group of panelists who are experts in their fields. In addition, BWLA has several committees where its members can work on various projects, learn from each other, share their opinions, develop policy initiatives within the legal community, etc.
**Structure:** varies depending on the event; might be roundtables or summits
**Extras:** For an additional fee, members can participate in BWLA Lawyers Referral Service. BWLA also gives out scholarships to deserving and needy law-school students.

**National Coalition of 100 Black Women** ($, N)
*http://www.ncbw.org/intro.html*
NCBW is a nonprofit organization present in Illinois (and twenty-three other states and the District of Columbia). Its mission is "the development of socially conscious female leaders who are committed to furthering equity and empowerment for women of color in the society-at-large, improving the environment of their neighborhoods, rebuilding their communities, and enhancing the quality of public and private resources for the growth and development of disadvantaged youths. NCBW is dedicated to community service, the creation of wealth for social change, the enhancement of career opportunities for women of color through networking, and strategically designed programs and the empowerment of women of color to meet their diverse needs."[25]
I have to mention that though the national Web page hasn't been updated since 2003 (by the looks of it), it contains a link to local chapter Web sites (or you can go directly to *http://www.ncbw.org/aboutus/aboutus.html*). Most of these local sites are up-to-date, which means the chapters are quite active. The

---

24   The information is from BWLA Web site
25   The information is from NCBW Web site

Illinois chapter doesn't have a Web site but has contact details for the chapter's president.

The events vary by chapter. Overall, they represent a wide spectrum from health related events (for example, an AIDS walk) to fundraising, to educational events, and to cultural and social events.

**Good for:** business and professional development, getting involved in the community activities, networking, etc.

**Extras:** You can start your own chapter in your area if there isn't one.

**Asian Women in Business** (membership $, events FREE and $, some services FREE, New York[26])
http://www.awib.org/awib.html

AWIB is a not-for-profit membership organization whose main goal is "to assist Asian women to realize their entrepreneurial potential. AWIB fills a vital need for women who need information, education, and networking opportunities to start or expand their businesses."[27] AWIB sponsors many conferences and workshops, provides individualized technical assistance, and serves as a support mechanism for small-business owners.

**Good for:** starting or developing business, professional development, networking, making friends

**Advantages:** Though this is a New York—based organization and all the events take place there, AWIB has some valuable resources available to women in Chicago. For example, AWIB offers a U.S. online directory of small businesses, which anyone (even nonmembers) can search for free. You can specify a state, a field (such as manufacturing, retail, services, etc.), and if you are looking for an Asian-owned business. Anyone can list his or her business in this directory for free.

**Structure:** AWIB organizes many types of events, including educational seminars (how to start a business), neighborhood events, trade fairs (holiday shopping with AWIB), holiday parties, etc.

*****Organization of Women in International Trade** ($, N)
*http://www.owit.org*
    See chapter 4 for more details.

---

26   Some services available nationwide

27   The information is from AWIB Web site

**Indus Women Leaders** (N, membership FREE, events $ and FREE)
*http://www.induswomenleaders.org*
Indus Women Leaders (IWL) is a national forum that develops South Asian women leaders. IWL provides South Asian women with the resources to achieve their life goals through goal-setting tools, advocacy, networking, mentorship, and education.

The IWL mailing list, Web site resources, and national events are available to all members regardless of state. Chicago is home to one of its five local chapters that organize local events. (Boston, New York, Washington DC, and San Francisco also have chapters.)
**Good for:** personal and professional development, networking, making friends
**Advantages:** this is a unique forum for South Asian women. IWL organizes social events (book clubs, culinary classes, etc.) and business events (workshops, lectures, networking sessions). It also organizes a yearly conference and runs a leadership award program. In addition, IWL promotes mentorship, peer-to-peer coaching, and peer advisory groups among women members.
**Structure:** varies depending on the event

**100 Hispanic Women** ($, NY)
*http://www.100hispanicwomen.org*
More information is provided in the next section of this chapter.

# ETHNIC GROUPS

It is commonly said that the United States is a country of immigrants. The size of minority ethnic groups is constantly growing due to immigration, and these minority groups naturally get together. The goals of the organizations in this subgroup vary. Some promote social interaction, some facilitate discussions of issues of interest (diversity, issues at workplace, etc.), and some assist in the development of minority-owned small businesses established on U.S. territory.

The **African American/Latino/Asian (ALA) roundtable at NAWBO** Chicago Chapter (see the section "Women's Organizations," earlier in this chapter) is an example of a group that unites members from several ethnic minorities. Here are examples dedicated to one specific ethnic group:

## African American

**African American Chambers of Commerce, ($, N)**

African American chambers of commerce can be found in most of states. Here are some samples of available links:

California: *http://www.calbcc.org*
Ohio/Kentucky: *http://www.gcaacc.com*
Oregon: *http://www.blackchamber.info/default.cfm*

The Chicago African American chamber of commerce does not currently have a website but you can find information you need by calling them at 773-238-3840.

The umbrella organization for all these local chambers is the National Black Chamber of Commerce (*http://www.nationalbcc.org*). According to its Web site:

> This business association represents 95,000 Black-owned businesses and provides an advocacy that reaches all one million Black-owned businesses. The NBCC is a nonprofit, nonpartisan, nonsectarian organization dedicated to the economic empowerment of African American communities. One hundred ninety affiliated chapters are locally based throughout the nation as well as international affiliate chapters based in Bahamas, Brazil, Colombia, Ghana, and Jamaica and Businesses.

**Black Contractors United ($, Ch)**
*http://www.blackcontractorsunited.com*
This organization unites African American-owned small businesses in the construction industry. Its mission is "to expand the basis of African American construction businesses; to assist African American contractors in achieving parity in the free marketplace without bias and prejudice; to provide quality professional, technical, and maintenance assistance; and to act as a liaison between the minority and majority contracting communities for the benefit of both".[28]
**Good for:** business development

---

28    The information is from BCU Web site

**Advantages:** In addition to providing all sorts of business support, BCU organizes several annual fun events, such as dinners, golf outings, and rodeos.

**Black Women Lawyers' Association of Greater Chicago** ($, Ch)
*http://www.bwla.org*
For information, see the "Women's Organizations" section earlier in this chapter.

**National Coalition of 100 Black Women** ($, N)
*http://www.ncbw.org/intro.html*
For information, see the "Women's Organizations" section earlier in this chapter.

**The Links Inc** (N, $)
*http://www.linksinc.org*
For information, see the "Women's Organizations" section earlier in this chapter.

For more listings of African American organizations in various industries and fields of interest, please visit the following Web site:
**African American Web Connection**
*http://www.aawc.com/Zaao.html*

# Asian

**Chicago Chinatown Chamber of Commerce** ($, Ch)
*http://www.chicagochinatown.org*
This is a great organization that not only helps small and medium-sized Asian businesses to develop and grow but also dedicates itself to promotion and development of Chinatown, a unique and beautiful area of Chicago. It is a very active chamber of commerce. It organizes a lot of business, educational, networking, and recreational (for example, the annual Chinese New Year celebrations) activities.

**Asian American Alliance** ($, IL)
*http://www.asianamericanalliance.com*
"The Asian American Alliance is a not-for-profit small business advocacy organization committed to assisting Asian American, minority, non-minority, women-owned small and disadvantaged business owners in Illinois.

"The Alliance was incorporated in 1994 as a result of collaborative efforts by the Chinatown, Korean, Philippine and Vietnamese American Chambers of Commerce."[29]

**Good for:** starting and developing business, educational purposes, making connections and friends

**Advantages:** Asian American Alliance runs a small-business development center that provides the following services (as listed on its Web site):

- Technical assistance to clients interested in starting up or expanding an existing business
- Information on governmental lending programs, available commercial lending sources, development of a business plan or other related services
- Training to inform the small business community of available governmental, private, and independent resources

Workshops are also organized on the following topics: business-plan development, women and investing, estate planning, and more.

**Structure:** mostly workshops, training seminars

### The National Association of Asian American Professionals (N, $)

*http://www.naaap.org*
*http://www.naaapchicago.org* (Chicago Chapter)

NAAAP is a not-for-profit organization where professionals of various Asian backgrounds work together across the country. It serves "to educate not only our members through professional development but also raise Asian American awareness in corporate America and ensure that Asian Americans are included in diversity programs."[30] NAAAP is present in major metropolitan areas of the United States and Canada in the form of chapters or ventures.

**Good for:** networking, making friends, getting actively involved in the community, business development, professional development

**Advantages:** NAAAP Chicago organizes various types of regularly scheduled events. Business and professional development events range from roundtables to conferences to networking extravaganzas. There are also community events: cultural activities such as documentary-film screenings, panel discussions, and volunteer community-service projects. Members can also be actively involved

---

29   The information is from the Alliance's Web site
30   The information is from NAAAP Web site

in several committees: community service, corporate relations, education, marketing, social and cultural, university relations, and more.

**Structure:** varies depending on the event

**Extras:** NAAAP Chicago organizes some ad-hoc events such as the Chicago Asian American Heritage Month Essay Contest (once a year in the spring) and the Chicago Community Leadership Scholarship contest (held for the first time in 2006).

**Filipino American Council of Greater Chicago** ($, Ch)

*http://www.faccrizalcenter.org/page/page/994753.htm*

This is the oldest Filipino organization in the United States. It serves the Filipino community in Chicago and the suburbs, and its services are social, cultural, and educational in nature. Services include: legal services, a food distribution program, dancing lessons, language classes, religious services, nursing review classes, etc.

The Filipino community is quite strong and united in Illinois, and there are a lot of Filipino organizations of various natures in this state. To see a full list, please visit the Filipino Network Web site at:

**The Filipino,** IL

*http://www.thefilipino.com/filipinosinillinois.html.*

For an exhaustive list of other Asian American organizations in the United States, please visit:

**Asian Women in Business** (see Women's Organizations, chapter 6, for more details)

*http://www.awib.org/content_frames/directory/asian*

## Hispanic (Latino)

**Illinois Hispanic Chamber of Commerce** (IL membership $, events $, some services FREE)

*http://www.ihccbusiness.net*

The Illinois Hispanic Chamber of Commerce works to provide resources to businesses as well as advocate on issues that affect the Hispanic business community. IHCC is committed to increasing the participation of Hispanic businesses in all commercial and economic areas.

**Good for:** business start-up, business and professional development, networking

**Advantages:** IHCC offers a number of free services to its members:

- Business development and start-up assistance
- Minority and disadvantaged business certifications
- Drug-free workplace training
- Procurement assistance

**Structure:** monthly members meetings that include networking and a presentation on a topic of interest

**\*Hispanic Alliance for Career Enhancement** (N, membership $, some services and events FREE)
*http://www.hace-usa.org*

HACE is a national nonprofit organization dedicated to "building Latino careers through leadership and career development of Latino students and experienced professionals and recruitment programs for the acquisition of this talent by leading corporations, the government and other institutional employers."[31] HACE is currently active in Illinois and four other states (New York, Florida, Texas, and California).

**Good for:** career transition, networking, and professional development.

**Advantages:** HACE members get access to exclusive job postings from leading corporations through its job bank. Members can participate at a discount rate in various networking events sponsored by HACE. HACE also offers its members special discounts on career-management and personal-skills workshops. HACE organizes Latino Recruitment Series events held at the offices of leading corporations that have an expressed interest in hiring Hispanic talent.[32]

**Structure:** varies depending on the event

**Extras:** HACE offers professional advice to its members on writing resumes and cover letters, negotiating salaries, and getting into postgraduate programs

---

31  The information is from HACE Web site

32  In my personal experience, these are the most powerful events for job seekers. Candidates have the opportunity to spend the whole evening (about three hours) at a company's headquarters. There is usually informal networking in the beginning, followed by a panel presentation, Q&A, and an opportunity to meet with representatives from various departments (IT, marketing, finance, HR, etc.) to discuss current openings with real people and leave resumes. These events are usually free of charge. Non-members and non-Hispanics can attend, too.

in business or law. It will provide a coach to help you create a career plan that is right for you.

**100 Hispanic Women, Inc. ($, New York)**
*http://www.100hispanicwomen.org*
100 Hispanic Women, Inc., is a not-for-profit organization established as a forum for Latinas, other individuals, and organizations who support Hispanas. The group provides a forum where people come together to address issues affecting our communities, influence public policy affecting Latinas and their families, and promote diversity. The goal of this organization is "to ensure that Latinas, through networking and aggressive outreach, achieve leadership positions which influence public policy and shape an equitable and humane society."[33]

Though this is currently a New York organization, it is now expanding to New Jersey and hopefully will soon reach other communities across the United States.

**Good for:** networking, professional and personal development, business development

**Advantages:** In addition to traditional networking events each year, 100 Hispanic Women organizes a series of symposia that cover topics from professional development and education to wealth management. The organization has attracted experts and influential Latinas to address its members.

Also, the organization is known for its yearly fall conference: "Mind, Body, and Spirit ... the Road to Serenity." The conference is designed as a therapeutic retreat for women to de-stress and deal with the challenges of conforming to the traditional Latina role and the demands of a professional career. Speakers (psychotherapists, sex therapists, health-food experts, and Yoga spiritualists) conduct interactive workshops. In addition, cosmetic company representatives illustrate makeovers and how to create "spa-at-home" treatments.

**Structure:** varies depending on the event

**Extras:** 100 Hispanic Women sponsors the Young Latinas Leadership Institute (YLLI), a program that provides young Latinas with the tools and support to pursue and attain college degrees. The aim of YLLI is to prepare young Latinas for positions of leadership through mentorship opportunities, as well as unique experiential learning initiatives.

---

33   The information is from 100 Hispanic Women Web site

# GAY AND LESBIAN

The gay and lesbian community in Chicago is quite big and active. Chicago is famous for its annual PRIDE Parade, which attracts thousands of tourists from all over the country and the world. Dozens of social, cultural, athletic, and political events are organized in conjunction with PRIDE month.

There are a lot of social and community organizations that provide services for this group, and most of them can be found in the following free publication:

**Alternative Phonebook**
*http://www.apb-chicago.com*
I would like to draw your attention to several prominent organizations.

**Chicago Area Gay and Lesbian Chamber of Commerce** ($, IL)
*http://www.glchamber.org*
The Chicago Area Gay and Lesbian Chamber of Commerce is a not-for-profit organization established "to promote the development and growth of successful business enterprises by persons who self identify as gay, lesbian, or bisexual or transgendered persons."[34]
**Good for:** networking, building connections, business development
**Advantages:** The organization encourages and promotes gay/lesbian/bisexual-owned businesses and organizes various events that help people in the community to interact and support each other.
**Structure:** varies depending on the event; ranges from business networking to holiday parties
**Extras:** Since 2006, the Chicago Area Gay and Lesbian Chamber of Commerce also undertook a task of recognizing and celebrating accomplishments of lesbian, bisexual, and transgender women in the community by organizing a yearly awards and gala dinner.

**Chicago Prime Timers** (Ch/N, membership $, events $ and some FREE)
*http://www.primetimersww.org/chicago*
Chicago Prime Timers is a social club that is a part of an international organization known as **Prime Timers Worldwide** (visit http://www.prime timersww.org.) There are chapters in twenty-nine states and Washington DC. The mission of Prime Timers is "to provide mature gay and bisexual men and

---

34   The information is from the Chamber's Web site

their admirers to come together in a supportive atmosphere to enjoy educational, social, and recreational activities."[35]

**Good for:** networking, social activities, making friends

**Advantages:** Prime Timers organizes about a dozen events per month for all interest groups. Activities include: neighborhood dining, Sunday brunches, potluck dinners, gourmet dining, wine and cheese parties, bicycling, bowling, stage plays, movies, bar nights, pinochle, hearts, computer shoptalk, AIDS Walk Chicago, Chicago historical tours, and vacation tours.

**Structure:** trips, sports events, and dinners. Some events are held in members' homes. You can host an event at your place if you want.

### The Stonewall Association of Illinois (IL, FREE)
*http://www.stonewallassociation.com*

The Stonewall Association of Illinois is a Naperville-based umbrella organization composed of men and women of all ages. Its mission is "to encourage a sense of community which promotes unity, self acceptance, support, the sharing of ideas and interests, and the building of a supportive network of friends though social activities."[36]

**Good for:** social activities, networking, making friends

**Advantages:** The Stonewall Association runs a number of free social groups that meet on regular basis and address various issues of interest. These include: the Stonewall Self-Help Support group, the Stonewall Social group, A Bridge to Ideas discussion group, the Stonewall Young Adult group and Coming out of Marriage group.

**Structure:** There are two main types of activities: discussion groups and social events. Social events include dinners, movie trips, etc.

### Children of Lesbians and Gays Everywhere (COLAGE) (N, FREE)
*http://www.colage.org*

COLAGE is a nonprofit organization with a mission of engaging, connecting, and empowering people to make the world a better place for children of lesbian, gay, bisexual, and/or transgender parents and families. Today, COLAGE is the only national organization in the world specifically supporting children, youth, and adults with LGBT parent(s). It has chapters in twenty-nine states, including Illinois, and also in Canada, England, and Sweden.

**Good for:** social activities, connecting with people, making friends

---

35  The information is from Prime Timers Web site

36  The information is from the Association's Web site

**Advantages:** COLAGE chapters provide local community support and fun for people of all ages with lesbian, gay, bisexual, and/or transgender parents. The age range of participants and the types of groups vary from chapter to chapter. Some chapters provide regular events, peer groups, or activities; others act as the primary source for information and resources in their local communities. Many of the groups also engage in leadership development and connect families to opportunities to speak on panels, work with the media, and/or do legislative activism. COLAGE also gives you the opportunity to start a local chapter and will provide you with the necessary support.

**Structure:** COLAGE offers a number of programs: Youth Leadership and Activism, Pen Pals, Advocacy, and 2nd Generation LGBT. You can also participate in panels and online communities. COLAGE offers academic opportunities and training.

**Extra:** COLAGE publishes a magazine, *Just for You.*

# CHAPTER 7:
# FOR ALL AGES

There are organizations, associations, and clubs for all age groups in Chicago and nationwide. These cover a wider range of topics. There are also age-specific groups that concentrate their activities around the interests of smaller audiences. These include two main categories, young and mature, and thus have a more targeted approach.

Here are some of these groups:

*Young Professionals of Chicago (Ch, $, some events are FREE for members)
*http://ypchicago.org/home/index.jsp*
   Young Professionals of Chicago is a not-for-profit organization that offers professional development, social networking, and philanthropic opportunities to its members. YPC is the premier networking destination for young professionals in the Chicagoland area.[37]
**Good for:** professional development, business development, connecting with people, making friends
**Advantages:** YPC organizes a lot of different events each month that suit all tastes and needs. On its Web site, YPC promises to set up the following events each year:

- Six CEO breakfasts
- Six entrepreneur evening events
- Six exclusive members-only outings

---

37   The information is from YPC Web site

- Four large social celebrations
- Three professional development classes

YPC also offers networking opportunities, monthly happy hours, a monthly dinner series, monthly civic/philanthropic programs, and quarterly sports teams.

**Structure:** This varies according to the event. There can be between 30 and 250 attendees per event. If you are going on your own, and you don't know anyone, YPC's Meet and Greet program organizes happy hours or coffee groups prior to events so that members can network before attending large events. Most events are after work hours except for CEO breakfasts, which take place in the mornings.

**Extras:** This is a powerful and energetic group. A lot of potential "future leaders" attend these events, and the presentations are usually very powerful. As a rule, a presenter is a CEO of a leading company in its industry.

**Under 35 Roundtable of NAWBO** (Ch, services FREE for members)
*http://www.nawbochicago.org*
  See chapter 6 for details.

**Jobs for Youth** (Ch, FREE)
*http://www.jfychicago.org*
  The mission of Jobs for Youth (JFY) is "to help young men and women between the ages of 17–24 from low-income families become a part of the economic mainstream; and, in the process, to provide the business community with motivated, job-ready workers. JFY's core program includes pre-employment training, job placement, GED instruction, and supportive services."[38]
**Good for:** education, professional development, job search
**Advantages:** If you have a child or children in this age range and you are worried about his/her future, or if you are a youth who would like guidance related to education and job placement, then this is a good place to start your journey. JFY organizes job fairs, breakfast leadership forums (where Chicago business leaders give presentations for youths on various topics), social events (such as Jazz for Youth), and more.

---

38   The information is from JFY Web site

JFY also runs the following programs:

- Work Readiness/Life Skills Workshop, which provides job-placement assistance for seventeen- to twenty-four-year-old high-school graduates and GED recipients
- GED Preparation Program, a three-month program to prepare seventeen- to twenty-four-year-olds to take the GED exam
- DCFS Alternative High School program for wards of the state
- Ex-Offenders Special Assistance, a program for clients with criminal backgrounds

**Structure:** varies depending on the event; FREE workshops are highly recommended

**National Association of Baby Boomer Women** ($, N, see chapter 6 for details)
*http://www.nabbw.com*

**Grey Hair Management** (N, membership $ for top management, FREE for middle management, events $)
*http://www.grayhairmanagement.com*
   The Gray Hair Management® corporate mission is "to help professionals get jobs. All of the activities are focused on this mission, whether it is to help organizations and recruiters find qualified candidates, provide members with networking events and job leads, or to help individuals secure their next position with Pathways Through Transition℠ Coaching program."[39] Grey Hair Management has chapters in Appleton, WI, Charlotte, NC, Detroit, Los Angeles, Nashville, Chicago, Houston, Austin/San Antonio, Philadelphia, St. Louis, and Milwaukee.
**Good for:** those in career transition
**Advantages:** Grey Hair Management organizes its events and activities for senior managers and executives with substantial work experience. The main type of event is a structured networking meeting that helps professionals share their needs with other people and generate leads. The Chicago chapter organizes three meetings a month. One meeting is usually held in the early morning, and two occur after work hours. This organization is a great help, especially if you are new to the United States and are unfamiliar with American rules of networking and job searching at this level.

---

39   The information is from Grey Hair Management Web site

**Structure:** structured networking events where everyone is gathered around a number of tables; at each table, everybody has about three minutes to speak and distribute resumes and handbills (a one-page description of you and your target companies)

**Extras:** Members receive regular e-mails from Grey Hair Management with job leads. The company claims to send out around fifteen hundred leads every month.

# CHAPTER 8:
# PROFESSIONAL
# ORGANIZATIONS

Whatever your profession, chances are there will be some sort of professional organization serving your needs and interests in the United States.

These organizations can be divided into two main categories:

1.  Big national associations
2.  Smaller professional networking groups

Both categories are great resources for professional development and career transition. There are resources to help you stay aware of the developments in your industry, continue your education, and meet likeminded people.

## NATIONAL ASSOCIATIONS

National professional associations usually have thousands of members and operate chapters in every state. These are likely to organize numerous events (including seminars, conferences, training sessions, and symposia) on a big scale. Sometimes they will have smaller events such as presentations by distinguished speakers over breakfast or lunch.

They also serve as a strong unified voice for all professionals in the industry, lobbying your interests at the government level. Membership in these organizations is likely to be more expensive than in any other organization, but it is worth it if your goal is enhancing your professional knowledge and skills. Some companies reimburse their employees for joining professional associations.

National associations work closely with educational institutions and provide their members with educational opportunities through these institutions as well as multiple publications (articles, monthly magazines, books, and newsletters) and Internet resources on their Web sites (online training, libraries, and useful links).

Finally, most of the associations have a career page on their Web sites where you can post your resume and look for a job (or post a job if you represent a company). In addition, while attending professional associations' events, you can meet those people who potentially have the job opening you want; i.e., this is your chance to avoid the HR department and engage in a conversation directly with managers, directors, and heads of divisions who might be looking for candidates (or you can make them remember your face and name until such a position appears).

Since most of national professional associations have, more or less, the same structure and similar missions and goals, I will first describe their common features. Then the extras, which are usually specific to each particular entity, will follow.

**Good for:** professional development, career advancement
**Advantages:** The big size of these associations determines the huge quantity and high quality of events organized. The scope of the events is very wide, and, most importantly, there will always be events dedicated to the advancements, innovations, new government regulations, etc. in your industry. They provide a great learning experience. The presenters at these events are usually outstanding and well known.

It is practically impossible to list all national professional associations, since there will be one for virtually every profession. Below is the list of some with notable extras.

**\*American Marketing Association**
*http://www.marketingpower.com*
**Extras:** American Marketing Association's Web site provides free, useful tools for practitioners (ROI calculator, demographic surveys, relocation information, marketing templates, salary surveys, etc.) and academics (research links, teaching opportunities, etc.).

## American Medical Association
*http://www.ama-assn.org*
**Extras:** American Medical Association provides a lot of free information on medical fellowships and residencies, legal issues, practice-management tools, medical ethics, and AMA advocacy efforts. In addition, a licensed doctor can have his or her name listed with AMA, and general public can search the online AMA database to find a doctor.

## *Institute of Management Consultants
*http://www.imcusa.org*
**Extras:** IMC puts a lot of stress on continuous education of consultants. Its Web site offers many educational tools, including a comprehensive consulting-fee analysis.

In addition to big events, local chapters organize smaller networking events. The Chicagoland chapter holds a monthly event for all chapter members (usually forty to fifty consultants attend) with a formal presentation and networking session. There are smaller events (ABC meetings, also held once a month) in Chicago neighborhoods where consultants (usually ten to fifteen people) from that area get together to network in an informal atmosphere. They engage in informal discussion on a certain topic, share experiences, etc.

## American Bar Association
*http://www.abanet.org*
**Extras:** ABA provides many free resources for legal-practice management, such as insurance, risk management services, and technology help. ABA has a strong, unified voice, but it is divided into many smaller groups (committees, divisions, sections, commissions, task forces, and centers) so members can find a niche depending on the type of law they practice and where their interests lie. For instance, you can get involved in the International Law division and the Client Protection Committee.

## American Teachers Association
*http://www.nea.org/events/ATA.html*
**Extras:** American Teachers Association merged with National Education Association, and now ATA members enjoy NEA benefits as well. ATA provides free valuable tools for teachers such as lessons ideas and classroom management advice. Members can share teaching experiences. The association also provides information on grants available to teachers.

The Illinois chapter offers resources for different subgroups within the teaching profession. There are resources for teachers, paraprofessionals, and students studying to become teachers (such as a mentoring program and student's advisory board). There are also chapters for retired teachers.

**American Bankers Association**
*http://www.aba.com/default.htm*
**Extras:** ABA helps its members to improve their performance by sharing best practices in the industry. ABA provides its members with free industry survey reports and peer-group benchmarking reports. It also has various resources and publications (Emergency Preparedness Toolbox, Bankruptcy Reform Guide, Fraud Communications Kit) available to its members.

**American Association for Clinical Chemistry**
*http://www.aacc.org/AACC*
**Extras:** AACC is comprised of various divisions and committees, and you can get involved in one or several of them depending on your field of interest. AACC has tailored services for experienced specialists and young "laboratorians." In addition, AACC organizes a monthly program called "Expert Access." These are live online discussions featuring a "hot topic" and an expert host. All participants can ask questions and get answers in real time.

**International Association of Business Communicators** ($, N)
*http://www.iabc.com*
*http://www.iabcchicago.com* (Chicago chapter)
    See chapter 4 for details.

It is likely that you can perform a Google search of the key words "American [Your Profession] Association" to find your professional organization if it is not listed here.

# PROFESSIONAL NETWORKING GROUPS

These groups are smaller and quite often local rather than national. Their main advantage is that they have a more personal approach. They are more focused on local communities and on the industries and job market in a particular state. These groups are numerous but more difficult to find. Sometimes they don't have Web sites, but sometimes you can contact them through a Yahoo! Group service or by e-mail. I learned that church employment councils (see chapter

2) or organizations for those in transition (which I will dwell upon in detail in chapter 9) usually have information about these local groups.

**Engineering Fellowship League** (Ch, FREE)
*http://personalresume.net/EngineeringFellowshipLeague*
The purpose of this group is "to provide a peer relationship, and safe harbor for anyone who creates things or has a direct relationship of those that create things using logic, mathematics, spatial assembly (CAD)."[40] They network and form accountability groups, have engineering discussions, and share information.

The group is composed of persons with engineering-related professions (industry non-specific). Members may have jobs in industrial and manufacturing engineering, facilities engineering, civil engineering, product design (artistic, ergonomics, marketing focus groups), mechanical engineering, electrical engineering, and research and development.

This group also welcomes you to open your own chapter(s) in other locations.

**Good for:** networking, career advancement or transition, general assistance
**Advantages:** You will meet likeminded people who know your industry and the job market for your profession. You can bounce ideas off each other and discuss topics of common interest.
**Structure:** monthly meeting with a presentation, discussion, and informal networking

**ChemPharma** (N, membership $, events FREE)
*http://www.chempharma.net*
ChemPharma is a nationwide networking organization for business and technical executives in the chemical, life science, pharmaceutical, and allied industries. ChemPharma's mission is "to foster an environment at the regional and national levels to promote effective networking and development for its members to assist in achieving one's career goals and business interests."[41]

At the moment, there are chapters of ChemPharma in Chicago, Boston, Philadelphia, and New Jersey.

**Good for:** networking, connecting with people, career advancement or transition
**Advantages:** ChemPharma allows you to link up with professionals and executives in the chemical and pharmaceutical industry for mutual exchange of ideas,

---

40   The information is from Engineering Fellowship League Web site

41   The information is from ChemPharma Web site

contacts, and lifetime friendships. In addition, ChemPharma offers numerous career advancement seminars and information for both members in search of new jobs as well as those that are presently employed and interested in managing their careers. Employers can submit their job openings, which will be e-mailed to all members. This is a free service.

**Structure:** Monthly meetings typically include a sixty-minute presentation on a subject relevant to the industry, career issues, or networking. The remainder of the meeting is used for formal networking. Several recruiters will periodically attend ChemPharma meetings to discuss positions that they are looking to fill.

### Marketing Executives Networking Group (N, $)
*http://www.mengonline.com*

MENG is a national network of senior marketing professionals devoted to "enhancing its members' professional careers, knowledge, relationships, businesses, and skills."[42] It provides information, education, resources, and networking opportunities.

MENG is currently present in eleven locations in the United States: Atlanta, Boston, Chicago, Connecticut, Dallas, Miami, New York, New Jersey, Northern and Southern California, Philadelphia, and Washington DC.

**Good for:** connecting with people, networking, career advancement, business development (in consulting)

**Advantages:** You have an opportunity to establish new connections and share industry expertise and trends. The organization mentions on its site that it is rather popular with recruiters. Your resume will have a lot of visibility, plus you will have access to their guide, "How to Conduct an Executive Level Job Search." In addition, all members get free access to its monthly job search "Webinar" series and business school/marketing trends "Webinars."

MENG markets itself as an ideal resource for businesses that require consultants or contact services. It heavily promotes members who have their own marketing consulting companies.

MENG has several special interest groups (depending on industry and marketing functions) that give MENG members an opportunity to address their special interests and needs. Each special-interest group (SIG) holds regular teleconferences, and some even stage occasional regional get-togethers. Each SIG has its own Web page, e-mail discussion list, and events calendar. Some of the SIGs are pharma, consulting, B2B, CPG, and media.

**Structure:** varies depending on the event; includes face-to-face meetings and regular teleconferences

---

42   The information is from MENG Web site

**Direct Selling Women's Alliance** (N, $)
*http://www.mydswa.org*
   See chapter 6 for details.

**Authors Marketing Group** (IL, membership $,[43] meetings FREE)
*http://www.authorsmarketinggroup.org*
   If you are a writer, this is a great organization for you. Its mission is "to provide a venue for Chicago-area authors to come together and share marketing ideas and experiences to help everyone sell more books."[44] The group accomplishes its goals through a substantive, informative Web site and newsletter, evening meetings with guest speakers, and other information-sharing activities.
   If you would like to explore this organization, you can come to your first meeting free before joining to see if it has something to offer you.
**Good for:** networking, connecting with people, making friends, learning how to publish and promote your books
**Advantages:** This is a great resource if you are beginning your career as an author. There is a lot of knowledge in this group.
**Structure:** Meetings are held once every two months and include a presentation, a discussion, and networking.
**Extras:** All authors get their own page on AMG's Web site where they can tell everything about their books, include pictures, etc.

**\*Consumer Products Group (CPG) Networking Group** (IL, FREE)
naglejc@aol.com[45]
   This is purely a networking group for people in transition with consumer-products backgrounds across a variety of functional areas including marketing, sales, finance, and operations.
**Good for:** networking, getting job leads, finding information about your industry and job market if you are in career transition
**Advantages:** This is a specialized and focused group with a mission of helping its members to become re-employed. From the pool of people (usually there are about fifty attendees per meeting), you can find out insider information about a company of interest and get leads and general support. Most of the people are sincere and helpful.

---

43   The fee is minimal.
44   The information is from the Group's Web site
45   This is one of the specialized groups that doesn't have a Web address. To register, you have to send an e-mail to the address indicated.

**Structure:** The group meets once a month at Schaumburg Public Library. The meeting is usually involves structured networking. Everyone around the table has two to three minutes to give an "elevator speech" and pass around resumes and handbills. You have a chance to change tables three or four times per meeting.

### *Business Network Chicago (BNC) (IL, FREE)
*http://www.bnchicago.org*

The BNC is a networking group for job seekers, entrepreneurs, and working professionals seeking to establish mutually rewarding relationships with like-minded individuals. Members meet in a fun, friendly, relaxed atmosphere to exchange ideas, share contacts, and invest in each other's success. Professional speakers are brought in to address all phases of a career. Active participants will acquire the education, tools, and networking skills needed to successfully find a job, start their own company, or manage their careers.

This is one of the friendliest and fastest-growing networking groups because of many factors. Its members are great people, its events are excellent, and membership and events are free to all.

BNC organizes monthly social events in the evenings and professional lunches. The professional lunch groups bring together people from the fields of advertising, sales and marketing, IT, HR, "C" level executives, entrepreneurship, health care, international business, and venture capital.

**Good for:** people in career transition, business development, networking, making friends

**Advantages:** For those in career transition, BNC members send each other dozens of job leads via e-mail every day. If you want to develop your leadership skills, you can set up your own professional luncheon group under the BNC umbrella

**Structure:** monthly lunches with structured networking and discussions of topics of interest; monthly evening social events with informal networking

### TECH Cocktail (Ch, FREE)
*http://www.techcocktail.com/blog*

TECH Cocktail offers a series of mixer events open to bloggers, technology enthusiasts, entrepreneurs, and other business professionals interested in the technology arena in Chicago and other underserved technology communities.

TECH Cocktail helps to create a place for bloggers, technologists, entrepreneurs, and other business professionals to meet, share ideas, and have some fun. TECH Cocktail is not exclusive to Chicago; its events are open to the public, and this group invites everybody to blog or podcast the events. Its goal is "to see the tech community better connected and recognized through TECH cocktail."[46]

This organization also opened a job board. Job openings in the technology sector can be posted and searched for free.

**Good for:** those in career transition, networking, socializing, meeting like-minded people

**Advantages:** TECH Cocktail is linked to Tech Social (www.techsocial.com), which posts social events for technologically minded people not only in Chicago but worldwide. Tech Social specializes in connecting Chicago's technology and entrepreneurship communities to interesting events. Technologists and business people who want to start businesses need to get out and meet each other. Tech Social facilitates this by providing an updated calendar of high-tech seminars, talks, clubs, meetings, meet ups, etc. Events posted on Tech Social are free and paid events.

**Structure:** varies depending on the event

**\*NAWBO (National Association of Women Business Owners)** (membership \$, events FREE and \$, N)
*http://www.nawbo.org*
*http://www.nawbochicago.org* (Chicago chapter)

NAWBO has a number of roundtables for professional special-interest groups. The Chicago-chapter roundtables are Windy City Investors, Creatives SIG (where everyone from advertisers to interior designers are welcome), and Spouses Business Partner Group (for NAWBO members and spouses who are also business partners). See chapter 6 for more details about NAWBO.

**Federation of Women Contractors**[47] (\$, Ch)
*http://www.fwcchicago.com/welcome.htm*
See chapter 6 for details.

**Black Contractors**[48] **United** (\$, Ch)
*http://www.blackcontractorsunited.com*
See chapter 6 for details.

---

46  The information is from TECH cocktail Web site
47  Construction industry
48  Construction industry

# CHAPTER 9:
# FOR THOSE IN CAREER TRANSITION

Relocation can be one of the most difficult times in a person's life. His or her company might not even have an office in the new city. The job market may be different, industries may be different, and the demand for professional staff might be different, too.

It is probably a hundred times more difficult when a person relocates to the United States from a different country. Add language and cultural barriers, and a whole new approach to job searching is required. In the United States, a lot of stress is put on networking in the job-search process. This is less true in the United Kingdom, where I was relocating from, and even less true in Russia, where I grew up.

The good news, however, is that even if you are coming from another country, there are a lot of resources here (job ministries, job clubs, etc.) to support you if you find the right places to go. Most importantly, most of these organization offer free services or require just a minimal charge.

Churches (N, FREE, see chapter 2 for more details)

I probably cannot stress enough that church communities in the United States are extremely helpful to people in career transition. They meet on a regular basis (usually once weekly or biweekly), their services are free, they have loads of useful information, and they will teach you everything from how to write a resume to what is a handbill and how to use it.

Information on church-based job-support groups can be found on http://www.workministry.com/job_support_groups.shtml. The Web site is a great help for job seekers, and it gives information on resources in twenty-five states and Washington DC.

*Business Network Chicago (BNC) (IL, FREE, see chapter 8 for more details)
*http://www.bnchicago.org*
Though with time BNC grew to include both job seekers and working people who would like to network, it was originally established as a support group for people in career transition. That is why it still has this strong mutual support and helpful atmosphere and provides a wealth of knowledge on job-seeking techniques, tips, etc. People come here from various industries and job functions. Recently, a number of recruiters joined the club, and they are now sending multiple job leads in e-mail blasts to all BNC members.

**Employing America** (IL, FREE)
*http://www.employing-america.com*
Employing America is a nonprofit organization dedicated to helping all unemployed and underemployed persons prepare to find employment.[49] Employing America, at no cost, serves all job seekers who must remain securely employed to support their families, churches, and communities. As mentioned on its Web site, EA dedicates its work to the following:

- Partnering with employers and organizations such as churches, government agencies, and local groups to provide support to job seekers
- Assisting individuals with special needs, including those who are bilingual, disabled, and/or senior citizens to find jobs
- Assisting faith-based, nonprofit organizations with establishing their own job networks
- Offering employers and organizations an alternative to recruiting employees

**Good for:** those in career transition
**Advantages:** EA provides the following services:

- Career counseling, planning, and interview coaching
- Job-skill coaching and resume reviewing
- Training seminars and job-related literature
- Web site for daily job posting, links to intranet of job resources, and a library of articles

---

49  Note: This is *not* a job-placement service.

- Centralized resource for coordinating information, schedules, and special events of area support groups
- Consultation and ongoing support to faith-based and nonprofit organizations who want to start their own job networks

On the EA Web site you can find a good list of church-based and non-church-based job ministries and clubs located throughout Illinois.

### Career Transitions Center of Chicago (Ch, $)
*http://www.ctcchicago.org*
CTC is an independent not-for-profit organization serving people in job or career transitions. It offers professional, emotional, and spiritual support to Chicago-area workers who have lost their jobs.
**Good for:** people in career transition
**Advantages:** CTC offers various services. Every client who registers gets a job coach. Job coaches can provide personalized one-on-one consultation with clients. They can help job seekers develop a clearer picture of the relationship between their qualifications, the requirements of their desired career directions, and plans for success. CTC has more than thirty coaches coming from different professional backgrounds to satisfy most needs, and it is up to you to choose a coach you are most comfortable with.
CTC organizes various workshops and seminars that help you develop the core skills for your job search. It organizes different networking events that can be attended by the general public. CTC also runs seminars for those who want to start their own businesses.
**Structure:** varies depending on the event
**Extras:** clients have access to sixteen cubicles with work space, telephones, and computers equipped with Microsoft Office software, Internet access via DSL high-speed links, and printers. The center is equipped with a copy machine, fax machine access, and a library with books, magazines, and newspapers to aid in your job search.

### Jewish[50] Vocational Services (Ch, $)
http://*www.jvschicago.org*
Founded in 1884 as a resource for Eastern European immigrants, the Jewish Vocational Service is an organization delivering a comprehensive selection of nonsectarian employment and training services. JVS assists a diverse population

---

50  You don't have to be Jewish to benefit from most of the career services JVS provides.

to explore career choices and find employment in a rapidly changing marketplace. People who benefit from these services include executives and middle managers, entrepreneurs, women returning to the workforce, young professionals, students seeking college counseling or scholarship assistance, refugees, persons with disabilities, and those who are economically disadvantaged.[51]

**Good for:** people in career transition, networking, connecting with people, education counseling

**Advantages:** JVS is quite a big organization with several offices in Chicago and its suburbs. It provides a number of services that can be divided into the following categories:

> *Career services* include workshops and seminars, networking events, career counseling, job-placement services, computer training, and access to a job resource center. Computer resources are available. Clients can conduct job-seeking research; create, print, or post resumes and cover letters; or work with knowledgeable staff in expediting an individual Internet job search. Publications highlighting the latest labor-market trends and effective job-campaign techniques are available.

> *Students' services* include college counseling and a possibility to win a college scholarship.

**Structure:** varies depending on the event

**Extras:** JVS also provides disability and refugee services. It offers zero- or low-interest micro-loans for small businesses.

**\*Executive Network Group of Greater Chicago** (IL, WI, IN $)
*http://www.engchgo.org*

ENG is a nonprofit organization that provides executives in transition with valuable resources and networking opportunities for finding new employment. Its mission is "to build networking and professional relationships among active members, ENG alumni, employers, executive recruiters, and other service providers and support groups.

"Drawing membership from a three-state area, this networking organization offers an incredible pool of proven management talent in all functional disciplines for both interim consulting projects and full-time positions."[52]

**Good for:** people in career transition, networking

---

51  The information is from JVS Web site

52  The information is from ENG Web site

**Advantages:** this group meets on a regular basis once every three weeks and usually attracts several dozen participants. Meetings have a good mixture of professional development and networking activities. ENG also offers recruiters free opportunities to place jobs on the ENG's Web site and search the site for resumes, which is a great incentive for recruiters to connect with the members of this networking group (which in turn speeds up the employment process)
**Structure:** Meetings usually run from noon to 4:30 PM. Each meeting has three parts: (1) the "pre-meeting" special interest groups, (2) a featured speaker, and (3) structured networking. Structured networking is within functional groups and then cross-functional groups.
**Extras:** ENG posts information on its Web site about various job-support groups in Illinois, Indiana, and Wisconsin. The link is:
http://www.engchgo.org/mmosdx/support/support_groups.php.

**\*Hispanic Alliance for Career Enhancement** (N, membership $, some services and events FREE)
*http://www.hace-usa.org*
   See chapter 6 for details.

**Grey Hair Management** (N, membership $ for top management, FREE for middle management, events $)
*http://www.grayhairmanagement.com*
   See chapter 7 for details.

**Jobs for Youth** (Ch, FREE, see chapter 7 for more details)
*http://www.jfychicago.org*

In addition to the organizations mentioned above, some of the groups described in chapter 8 also provide career transition services. Among these are: ChemPharma, Consumer Packaged Goods Group, and Marketing Executives Networking Group.

Most of these organizations are Illinois[53] specific, but if you do a Google or local search with such key words as "career (transition) center," "job ministry," or "job group," you will find resources in other states.

---

53   For more Illinois job-search support organizations, see Appendix 1.

# CHAPTER 10:
# FOR ENTREPRENEURS

If you, like me, relocated to a new place and decided to start your own business, then this is the chapter for you. The United States supports entrepreneurship like no other country in the world. If you are playing with the idea of becoming an entrepreneur, there is no better place to make it a reality.

The amount of support services for entrepreneurs in the United States is enormous, and it is impossible to list all of them. In this chapter, I will introduce just a small selection. All the existing organizations in this field can be categorized into two main groups:

1.  Organizations that provide educational, advisory, financial and start-up services for beginners
2.  Organizations (sometimes called "leads groups") that help you develop an existing business through networking and leads generation

## ADVISORY AND SUPPORT SERVICES

**Chicagoland Entrepreneurial Center** (IL, FREE[54])
*http://www.chicagolandec.org*
  The Chicagoland Entrepreneurial Center is a nonprofit affiliate of the Chicagoland Chamber of Commerce, whose goal is "to make a perceptible and lasting economic impact on the Chicagoland region by helping entrepreneurs and high-growth businesses build viable, sustainable, and profitable enterprises."[55]

---

54  The Web site doesn't mention any fees, so I assume it's free, except for the fees one has to pay to become a member of Chicagoland Chamber of Commerce.

55  The information is from the Center's Web site

CEC assists clients through one-on-one advisory services in financing and securing clients, capacity-building programs, peer-to-peer exchanges through service and educational opportunities offered by the center, and educational workshops and grants.

**Good for:** business development, professional development

**Advantages:** CEC helps with the theoretical part of business development—for instance, sales diagnostics, channel and market analysis, corporate positioning and messaging, sales pitch, and presentation coaching. It also helps with the practical parts of leads generation, targeted introductions to prospective clients, applications for loans, etc.

**Structure:** varies from workshops to networking events

Overall, all chambers of commerce have small-business development as one of their main objectives. They organize educational, networking, and promotional events for local businesses. For a full list of Chicago-area chambers of commerce, please see chapter 5.

**DePaul University Coleman Entrepreneurship Center** (Ch, events FREE and $)
*http://cec.depaul.edu*

The mission of DePaul CEC is "to help entrepreneurs succeed through exceptional assistance, valuable linkages, and innovative thinking."[56] The center offers specialized consulting services, educational programs, and helpful resources to entrepreneurs at different stages of the "Entrepreneurial Quest":

- EXPLORE for entrepreneurs planning to start, or buy, a business
- LAUNCH for entrepreneurs in the early stages of business, working to ensure sustainability
- GROW for entrepreneurs whose ventures are growing or are pursuing growth
- EVOLVE for entrepreneurs facing changes in ownership, personal involvement, or business model

**Good for:** business development, professional development, educational opportunities

**Advantages:** CEC offers consulting services such as: marketing-plan or business-plan development, feasibility studies, research studies, and business audits. It also organizes various monthly workshops and seminars (titles include Start Your Own Business, Start Your Non-Profit Organization, Prepare Your

---

56    The information is from the Center's Web site

Business for a Seamless Transition in Management). In addition, CEC designed a structured-networking program called "kNetworking for kNowledge" for entrepreneurs to begin building relationships. DePaul University also offers an academic program in entrepreneurial studies.

**Structure:** varies depending on the event

### GSB Entrepreneurial Roundtable (Wheaton, IL, FREE)
*http://www.gsbroundtable.com*

The Entrepreneurial Roundtable organizes monthly presentations on topics of interest for people who plan to start or buy a business, who already run a small or medium-sized business, or who are generally interested in learning more about entrepreneurism.

**Good for:** business development, connecting with likeminded people

**Advantages:** all presentations are free to the general public

**Structure:** monthly presentation (usually from a fellow successful entrepreneur) followed by a discussion and networking

### SCORE (N, FREE)
*http://www.score.org*

SCORE, "Counselors to America's Small Business," is a source of free and confidential small-business advice for entrepreneurs. SCORE chapters can be found in all states, and there are usually several chapters in each state (depending on the size of the state).

**Good for:** business development, professional development, educational opportunities.

**Advantages:** SCORE offers "Ask SCORE" e-mail advice online, face-to-face small-business counseling at chapter offices, low-cost workshops at chapter officers, and useful online tools such as "how to" articles and business templates.

**Extras:** SCORE offers entrepreneurs the services of its business information centers at chapter officers. In the center, you can get free access to technology (computers with Internet access, business-planning and desktop-publishing software, printers and copy machines, etc.) and a library of resources (business, professional, and trade association directories; professional and business journals; and step-by-step guides for starting over 150 businesses).

### Asian American Alliance ($, IL, see chapter 6 for more details)
*http://www.asianamericanalliance.com*

**Illinois Hispanic Chamber of Commerce** (IL membership, events $, some services FREE)
*http://www.ihccbusiness.net*
    See chapter 6 for details.

**Women's Business Development Center** ($, Ch)
*http://www.wbdc.org*
    See chapter 6 for details.

These are just a few examples of small-business development organizations. The full detailed list for the whole state of Illinois (organized by region and county) can be found at:

**Illinois Department of Commerce and Economic Opportunity**
http://www.ildceo.net/dceo/Bureaus/Entrepreneurship+and+Small+Business/ Illinois+Entrepreneurship+Network+Directory/

# LEADS/NETWORKING GROUPS

Leads/networking groups exist all over the United States and around the world. Some of them are international and widespread; others are very local. But all of them have one mission: to help you achieve your goals through networking. Leads groups specifically concentrate on networking for business development. Other networking groups may also include career networking.

The main idea of a leads group is to unite a group of people from different professions on a regular basis. Some groups meet once a week, while others may meet only once a month. Only one representative from a professional field is allowed. Attendees get to know each member's business very well and help promote each other's businesses. Some leads groups are very formal; you have to come to each meeting with at least three leads for other people. Others are less formal, operating like a discussion forum and idea-generating team.

**BNI** ($, worldwide)
*http://www.bni.com*
    BNI is a large international business networking organization. It offers members the opportunity to share ideas, contacts, and, most importantly, business referrals. BNI has several chapters in each city (since only one person from each professional specialty is permitted to join a chapter of BNI).
**Good for:** business development, networking

**Advantages:** This is a very rigorous organization. It demands attendance at each meeting (usually held weekly, and if you cannot attend you have to send a substitute). You must also bring in valuable referrals for other members of the group. In addition to weekly events, BNI chapters organize social events where several chapters can be brought together and free periodic workshops (for example, leadership training). Different educational materials on networking and business-referral marketing are available to BNI members.

**Structure:** BNI events represent structured networking where everyone is given time for an elevator speech, and then there is time dedicated for providing leads to each other.

**Extras:** BNI members get free listings on the BNI Web site trade directory.

### Le Tip International ($, N)

*http://www.letip.com*

Le Tip International, Inc. is "a professional organization of men and women dedicated to the highest standards of competence and service. [Its] primary purpose is to give and receive qualified business tips or leads. Members will, at all times, maintain the highest professional integrity. Each business category is represented by one member and conflicts of interest are disallowed."[57]

Le Tip has chapters in twenty-three states, including Illinois, and Canada, and each city has several chapters (similar to BNI, described above).

**Good for:** business development, networking

**Advantages:** This organization is similar to BNI. You have to attend weekly meetings and bring at least four referrals per month for other members. But whereas BNI has very straightforward networking meetings, Le Tip has numerous rules, traditions, and even fines[58] for certain things. Depending on what type of networking you prefer, these differences may be valuable extras or little nuisances. More information on these extra rules can be found on Le Tip's Web site in the Q&A section.

**Structure:** Le Tip events represent structured networking where everyone is given time for an elevator speech, and then time is dedicated for providing leads and tips.

---

57   The information is from Le Tip Web site

58   Fines are usually of a small value.

**Ryze** (FREE, worldwide)
*http://www.ryze.com*

"Ryze helps people make connections and grow their networks. You can network to grow your business, build your career and life, find a job and make sales, or just keep in touch with friends.

Members get a free networking-oriented home page and can send messages to other members. They can also join special networks related to their industry, interests, or location. More than a thousand organizations host networks on Ryze to help their members interact with each other and grow their organizations."[59]

**Good for:** networking, connecting with people, business development

**Advantages:** Ryze has thousands of members all over the world. Its events Web page lists events for every day in every location. All members can post events for free. More than 50 percent of events are held in the United States. Ryze also has dozens (if not hundreds—I couldn't really estimate the number) of networks, which are interest groups devoted to a particular industry, profession, occupation, etc. Each network has its own events and forum-like discussion board, which you can join, or you can start your own network for free. There are currently three Ryze networks in the Chicago area. This is a good network for social interaction as well because people post their personal interests in their profiles.

**Structure:** varies depending on the event

**Extras:** Ryze publishes classified ads on its Web site, and you can post an ad for free.


**Business Builders Forum** (IL, $)
*http://www.bb4m.com*

Business Builders Forum is "forming business referral networks in many cities for enthusiastic business owners."[60] This organization aims to teach you how to create a properly working leads group in your area to help you and other group members develop their businesses. Business Builders Forum activities include weekly referral groups and monthly meetings:

-    BBF encourages business people to start up a BB4M weekly referral group with its assistance. They'll show you how to boost your attendance and make this hour a source of new business for all members.

---

59    The information is from Ryze Web site

60    The information is from BB4M Web site

- Monthly networking meetings provide a business topic, a chance to learn, and always include a "Power Networking" session. Bring your business cards, and come to network and make strategic partnerships. All area referral groups are welcome to attend the MAP meetings.

Currently, BB4M has fourteen referral groups in Illinois. Its ambition is to develop into a national organization.

**Good for:** business development

**Advantages:** BB4M has a structured approach to business development: weekly meetings where members are strongly encouraged to bring in good leads for others, monthly events, and a quarterly "super-networking event" called "Introduce My Company," where you are guaranteed to meet twenty other good business owners.

**Structure:** Weekly events are structured formal networking sessions. Other events' structures vary.

**Extras:** BB4M helps you grow your business through listing your company on a Web sites **http://www.Shoppers4M.com**, a national business directory that is "localized" (this means that every business is seen by the local consumers in your area).

### The Executives Club of Chicago (Ch, $)

*http://www.executivesclub.org*

The Executives Club of Chicago supports the Midwestern economy by "bringing Chicago's business community together with global leaders and practices at work in companies around the world; by helping organizations establish productive new business relationships in global markets."[61] Though members of this organization are predominantly in middle to upper management or are senior executives, ECC has a special forum for young professionals, too.

**Good for:** business development, professional development, connecting with people

**Advantages:** To help Executives Club members connect with the people most likely to impact their businesses, ECC has established nine committees. These committees develop programs or briefings focusing on specific topics and provide a forum for ECC members to network with others who share their special interests. Current committees and interest groups are: civic affairs, communications, finance, international, professional, reception, real estate, technology, and young leaders. The programs organized by ECC are diverse with local

---

61   The information is from the Club's Web site

and global impact. Examples of events are: Fortune 500 CEO Luncheon Series, Chicagoland CEO Breakfasts Series, and Women Leadership Breakfasts.

**Structure:** varies depending on the event

**Extras:** Members are invited to join trade and investment missions to key foreign markets and club briefings with senior government officials in Washington DC.

**Lincoln Park Network** (Ch, $)
*http://www.lincolnparknetwork.com*

This is an example of a very local network that operates in the Lincoln Park area of Chicago. The Lincoln Park Network is a referral, or "leads," group made up of independent professionals who share the common goal of helping one another's businesses grow and prosper.[62] Its members regularly discuss issues and brainstorm problems common to small businesses. As a group, LPN belongs to the Lincoln Park Chamber of Commerce.

**Good for:** business development, networking

**Advantages:** The group meets once a week for leads generation and also organizes evening social networking events. As a local organization, it helps local businesses to grow. LPN builds very close relationships, and even if you leave the network for any reason, LPN will list your name on its alumni Web page and even put a link to your business. For prospective members, LPN posts the categories (professions or businesses) currently unrepresented in its group.

**\*NAWBO (National Association of Women Business Owners)** (membership $, events FREE and $, N, see chapter 6 for details)
*http://www.nawbo.org*
*http://www.nawbochicago.org* (Chicago chapter)

Among other activities, NAWBO strongly supports the creation of leads groups by its members. Participation in the groups is free for members. These groups usually meet once or twice a month. Though they are strict in terms of having just one representative from each profession, they are more informal on the networking side.

There is no obligation to bring a certain amount of leads each time, though regular participation in the group is requested. These leads groups put more emphasis on building friendships and supporting long-lasting relationships. When members get to know each other better, they start helping each other to grow professionally and to grow their businesses based on the closeness of relationships within the group, not obligation.

---

62   The information is from LPN Web site

There are usually several leads groups within each chapter (based on geographic location). There are ten groups in Chicago and its suburbs (as of December 2006), and members are encouraged to create new groups if there is none in their area.

**Network of Women Entrepreneurs** (Ch, $))
*http://www.nwe-chicago.com*
    See chapter 6 for details

# CHAPTER 11:
# EDUCATIONAL
# ORGANIZATIONS

## LANGUAGE SCHOOLS

In my experience, language schools are extremely helpful for newcomers to the United States. Nothing makes you feel more like an alien in another country than not being able to communicate with people, and these schools offer places to brush up on your language skills. Language schools are also great places to make friends because the majority of people in your group will be in similar circumstances—most likely new to the country, without many friends or connections, and trying to figure out what they are going to do in this new place. Every person I know in Chicago who came from abroad and went to a language school upon arrival met at least one good friend there.

What if your English is great? Well, if you have some free time, study another language—say, Spanish, which is very popular in the United States—and make friends in your class. Learning a foreign language will never be a waste of time for your future and your career.

If you don't want to study a language but you feel lonely, you can still go to a language school where they teach your native language and meet with the teachers. They will most likely be your countrymen and, more often than not, will be glad to provide you the information about where your countrymen meet, shop, eat, and have fun.

There is one more advantage: it is never difficult to find a language school in a major city. They are plentiful. You may just have one on your doorstep.

When I came to the United States, I started brushing up on my French by going to the events organized by:

*Grouppe Professionel Francophone ($, Ch, see chapter 3 for more details)
*www.gpfchicago.org*
This is not a language school, but this organization is great for two reasons: improving language skills and business networking.

# UNIVERSITIES/COLLEGES

Local universities and colleges are helpful in two ways:

1. Most will organize various events that are open to the general public. These may be networking, educational, or professional-development events or a combination of all three.
2. Some will have services and resources available to the public that may be especially helpful for entrepreneurs.

You can attend events at a college or university for personal or professional development (i.e., as a purely educational opportunity). You may use these events as a field for networking—finding customers, partners, or even future colleagues. Many representatives of different companies (some of which you might be targeting in your job search) will attend these events. Potentially, this is a good opportunity to meet managers and heads of departments who might have an opening in the field you are interested in (instead of going through a human-resource department). And if these companies don't have openings at the moment, you can impress their representatives with your skills and abilities, helping them remember your face and business card till a suitable position opens in the future.

Here are some examples:

**Kellogg School of Management at Northwestern University** (Ch, events $)
*http://www.kellogg.northwestern.edu/difference/culture/conferences.htm*
KSM in Evanston, IL, is famous for organizing dozens of exciting conferences each year that attract professionals from all over the world and are open to the public for a fee. (The fee is minimal for students.) Topics range from biotechnology and healthcare to real estate. These conferences are educational and provide opportunities for networking and professional development. For more information on Kellogg's conferences, please visit the Web site listed above.

**University of Illinois at Chicago** (Ch, events FREE or $)
*http://www.uic.edu/htbin/eventcal/eventcal.fcgi*
The university's events Web page is a good resource. You can search multiple events by category (continuing and professional education; lectures, seminars, and meetings; etc.) Some events are free, while others require a fee for participation.

**DePaul University Coleman Entrepreneurship Center** (Ch, events FREE and $
*http://cec.depaul.edu*
See chapter 10 for more details

All colleges and universities have career departments helping their students and alumni find employment. Some will have resources on their Web sites that are available to the general public. As an example, the **Department of Neurobiology at University of Chicago** has more than twenty helpful links for people looking for a job in the science field. You can access its Web site at *http://pps.bsd.uchicago.edu/postdoc/career.html*.

These multiple resources available at educational institutions are often overlooked because the general public assumes that they are for current students or alumni only. In reality, you can benefit quite a bit if you take time to browse through the Web sites of major universities and colleges in your area. You will find many social, educational, and professional-development opportunities and business and sports activities organized on their premises that are open to the public.

# OTHER EDUCATIONAL ORGANIZATIONS

There are educational centers where you can learn anything from sports to craftsmanship to basic business skills. The great thing about these centers is that you are placed in a group of people with similar interests or hobbies, which makes it much easier to connect with people and make friends.

Chicago Discovery Center (Ch, $)
*http://www.discoverycenter.cc*
The Chicago Discovery Center offers a variety of classes, indoor and outdoor, with topics ranging from languages to dancing to skiing to personal growth. For those who are new to the United States, there is a useful selection

of classes in categories such as careers, business, and even friends and lovers (i.e., how to find friends or dates).

If you go to the Discovery Center's "affiliates" Web page, you will find links to similar learning centers across the United States.

# CHAPTER 12:
# OTHER ORGANIZATIONS
# AND ACTIVITIES

In this chapter I would like to talk about organizations and events that do not fit into any of the previous categories in this book but offer great opportunities for networking, connecting with people, developing a business, and making friends.

**Networlding** (Ch, $)
*http://www.networlding.com*
Networlding is a business-leadership, event-marketing, training, and coaching organization. Networlding provides a "seven-step" system for networking that "creates an acceleration of goal achievement."[63] Additionally, the unique Networlding community "enables its members to create successful professional relationships for business development, marketing, and leadership growth. Networlding builds value-based networks that help grow your business and your career to create a lifetime of success. Networlding helps people realize transformational opportunities."

Networlding organizes various events that teach you how to network properly (for business development, career enhancement, or other purpose) and then gives you opportunities to network. Its owner, Ms. Melissa Giovagnoli, published a number of books that teach the "Networlding" concept and how to succeed using it.
**Good for:** networking, connecting with people, business development
**Advantages:** Networlding has its own Leadership Resource Center, which offers the services of an integrated team of collaborative consultants, coaches, marketing,

---

63   The information is from Networlding Web site

and business-development specialists. It runs a special philanthropic program for young leaders (ages twenty-one to thirty) where these young professionals can get relevant coaching for just $10 an hour.

Networlding organizes not only big events (with a presentation, discussion, and networking) but also small, intimate roundtables that help you grow your leadership skills and provide you with the opportunity to network with other leaders interested in similar topics.

**Extras:** Networlding provides you with many free networking resources in the "What's New" section of its Web site.

# NETWORK MARKETING COMPANIES

Network marketing companies base their business growth model on building networks, and by default they organize a lot of events (which are usually free) to attract new people into their teams and promote their products. You don't need to join their businesses or buy their products, but attending a couple of events will teach you networking, give you opportunities to meet other people, and very often let you just enjoy yourself.

Not all network marketing organizations are the same, and not all of them are good for networking. A lot depends on the leader of the team whose event you attend. But one stands out:

* **Mary Kay** with Valerie Beck (Ch, events FREE and $)

One of the greatest entrepreneurial women and networkers I've ever known, Valerie Beck takes networking to the next level. Each MK event she organizes is in a great location; gives you an opportunity to learn about skin care, MK products (which you can try), and the company itself; and, of course, allows you to network. Every person attending an event has a chance to introduce herself,[64] tell what she does, and meet other women. Mary Kay events are free, and several are organized each month.

Ms. Beck has two other enterprises: Chicago Chocolate Tours and Romance Around the Corner. Sign up for a **Chicago Chocolate Tour**, and you will go on a sweet tour of Chicago's Michigan Avenue and have fun with other people in your tour group.

**Romance Around the Corner** is a series of seminars organized by Ms. Beck based on her book with the same title. These seminars will teach you "how to

---

64   The majority of MK event attendees are women.

get a man of your dreams and have fun in the process." They usually take place after working hours in a nice bar or café. Chocolate Tours and Romance seminars are paid events.

Best of all, if you attend one of Beck's events, you will be added to her e-mail distribution list. In the beginning of each month, you will receive her calendar of events, where she lists all events related to her three enterprises and other events of interest. In my experience, all of Valerie's events are friendly and fun, they are good for business networking and making friends, and most are specifically tailored for women.[65] Any of these events can be a perfect "girls' night out."

Ms. Beck's enterprises and their Web sites are interconnected. Through the Romance Around the Corner Web site, you can access information about Mary Kay business and events. The address is *http://www.romancearoundthecorner. com/mary-kay*.[66] You can find the link to Chicago Chocolate Tours on the same Web site.

## * Career Coaches (N, $)

If your goal is to find employment after relocating to the United States, and you are not sure if you can do it on your own in an unfamiliar country, then you need help from a specialist. In the United States, there are plenty career and life coaches who work for big companies or are independent consultants. I meet a lot of them while networking.

Fortunately, my former employer contracted with Spherion to provide a range of career transition services for me when I arrived in Chicago. Spherion was a fantastic help. I was their client for a year and they have been great. They provided consulting support, excellent on-line resources, teleconference type training modules, a database of resources on everything from how to write a resume to how negotiate a salary, and an ocean of information on nearly every company one might want to target in their career search. Spherion contracts with corporate clients to provide career transition services to employees and former employees. It Web site is: *http://www.spherion.com/corporate/home.jsp*

---

65    Chicago Chocolate Tours is great for both male and female chocolate lovers.

66    From this Web site, you can get information on all other events and activities.

# GOLF

If you are not American and especially if you are a woman, you will tend to underestimate the importance of golf. Here, it is more than a sport or a social occasion; it is a powerful business-building tool. Sarah L. Ferguson, a contributor to *Business First of Louisville* magazine, published a great article called "Ladies' tee time: Doing business on the course." The main idea of the article is that "building relationships, networking, and having 'face time' with clients are among the reasons for the growing number of women golfers."

Golf is a way to get included. In the article, Brenda Daniels, the pro at Quail Chase Golf Club, is quoted as saying: "Some women want to learn to play golf because they're tired of being 'golf widows.'" Others are taking up the game to play with their friends. "I had one woman who wanted to learn how to play because she was tired of being left out [of office scrambles]," said Daniels in the article.

Golf is also a business and networking tool. "Playing golf has business advantages ... because it gives a chance to develop personal relationships as well as business relationships with clients. Golf is a shortcut to figuring out whether you like someone personally and professionally," Suzanne Woo, a lawyer who owns BizGolf Dynamics, is quoted as saying in the article. "The golf course is a place where women and men can communicate without sexual innuendo." In the article, she admits that women are afraid of looking foolish, so she encourages beginners to take lessons and to learn golfing "etiquette."

The full article was published on *http://www.bizjournals.com/bizwomen/ louisville/content/story.html?story_id=889864.*[67]

From my own experience, I can say that in many organizations to which I belong the "golfing day out" is one of the biggest networking events of the year. This is true for the Chicagoland Chamber of Commerce, the National Association of Women Business Owners, and the Professional Women's Club of Chicago, to name just a few. So, if you don't want to be left out, you have to start playing golf in America.

To find extensive information on Chicago-area golf courses, golf schools, and driving rangers, visit *http://www.golfchicago.com*

If you are new to golf and want to learn more about etiquette, techniques, and (most importantly) how to socialize, capitalize, and network while golfing, one organization in Chicago offers special workshops for women covering all

---

67  This article was published in 2004, and we cannot guarantee that it will still be available on the Web.

these topics. Golf course practice time is available as well. You can learn all the necessary basics in a fun and friendly atmosphere at:

**Business on the Golfcourse** (Ch, $)
*http://www.businessonthegolfcourse.net*

## VOLUNTEERING

Volunteering is a great way to become involved with the community, get to know new people, and improve your language skills while you are in career transition or waiting for your U.S. work permit. Volunteering provides an alternative to sitting at home doing nothing.

Volunteering does not have to mean feeding animals at a shelter or cleaning rooms in a hospital. You can still do what you love—your job—but without being paid. If you are, say, a marketing professional, you can help a charity with its marketing communications or fundraising campaigns. In this way, you will not lose your business skills, you will definitely learn new marketing tricks (there is always a learning curve at a new job), and this experience will always look great on your resume.

# CHAPTER 13:
# INTERNET RESOURCES

In this chapter, you can find free online resources that list daily events in Chicago or nationwide. From business networking to career enhancement to social activities—you can find what you need if you know where to look. To access information on these sites, you need to register with them, but registration is always free.

**The ProNetworker** (IL)
*http://www.thepronetworker.com*
   This online resource is great for expanding business relationships. The site has a calendar that lists events, which are predominantly business development events or events for those in career transition, in Chicago and its suburbs. This is a very extensive resource; there may be up to thirty events listed per day.
   On this Web site, you can also find useful articles that will teach you how to network successfully.

**Global Chicago** (Ch)
*http://www.globalchicago.org/calendar/month_calendar.asp*
   This site lists all events with international flavor happening in Chicago. It is very well structured. You can search for events by category: cultural, business, academic, environment, government, etc.
   If you are member of Global Chicago (membership is free) you can post your events on this site for free.

Tech Social (worldwide)

*http://www.techsocial.com*

Tech Social specializes in "connecting Chicago's technology and entrepreneurship communities to interesting events."[68] The majority of events on this site are IT related and take place in Chicago, but you will also find occasional posts about events across the United States and worldwide.

When you register with this site, you will be able to submit your events, too.

TechVenue (worldwide)

*http://www.techvenue.com*

TechVenue positions itself on its Web site as the "official business technology events calendar." It is an online calendar of worldwide technology-related business events (face-to-face and online) organized geographically in an easy-to-use format. Events are listed globally by region. The number of events posted depends on the size of each state.

The events posted are of a diverse nature and include recruiting events, classes, networking events, seminars, etc.

Anyone can post an event to this Web site.

Meet Up (worldwide)

*http://www.meetup.com*

Meet Up is a unique Web site that provides information on various interest groups across the world, including in the United States. Within a twenty-mile radius of Chicago, the site shows more than five hundred top interest groups ranging from arts to pets, books, health, crafts, parenting—whatever your interest or hobby might be.

You can also perform a search of the largest and newest groups. The "largest groups" classification will show you the number of group members.

When you click on the name of an interest group, you will get information on its calendar of events and members.

This is an excellent resource for a newcomer because it helps people find others who share their interests or causes and form lasting, influential, local community groups that regularly meet face-to-face. These groups help you develop your social life in a new place and make friends.

---

68    The information is from Tech Social Web site

**ChicagoBusiness** (Ch)
*http://chicagobusiness.com/cgi-bin/calendar.pl*
   ChicagoBusiness is a Web site of a popular Chicago newspaper, *Crain's ChicagoBusiness*. Its calendar lists business-related events in Chicagoland. Events vary. Examples of events you can find in this calendar[69] include: College of DuPage CEO series, Table of 12 Reception (a reception to promote twelve local nonprofit organizations), Business Basics seminar: Starting a Business, and a workshop for women called "Secrets of Successful High Earners: Going to the Next Level in Your Life."

**Employing America** (IL, see chapter 9 for more details)[70]
*http://www.employing-america.com*
   Employing America is a nonprofit organization dedicated to helping all unemployed and underemployed persons prepare to find employment. EA provides a list of church-based and non-church-based job ministries and clubs located throughout Illinois. It shows dates, times, and places where these groups meet.

**Work Ministry** (N, see chapter 2 for more details)
*http://www.workministry.com/job_support_groups.shtml*
   The Web site is a great tool for job seekers. It gives information on church groups in twenty-five states and Washington DC. The mission of the organization is to help people find employment.

**Women for Hire** (N)
*http://www.womenforhire.com*
   This is a provider of career-advancement services for professional women. On the Web site, you can find some networking resources, blogs, and advice, but the biggest achievement of this organization is organizing nationwide career expos and early-morning seminars (held before the job fair itself) tailored specifically for women. A good number (approximately thirty to forty) of big companies usually participate in these expos.

**Chicago Job Fairs** (Ch)
*http://www.chicagojobresource.com/jobfairs.htm*
   This Web site provides a monthly calendar of dozens of job fairs, career fairs, employment fairs, and open houses organized by various organizations in Chicago and suburbs.

---

69  In most cases, events in this calendar do not overlap with the ProNetworker, so both Web sites are equally useful.

70  Also see Appendix 1 for Illinois job-clubs listings

**Monster** (N)

*http://monster.nationalcareerfairs.com/*

This is a good resource for job seekers. Monster organizes nearly three hundred job fairs each year across the United States, and all the information about dates and locations can be found on its Web site.

**LinkedIn** (worldwide)

*http://www.linkedin.com*

LinkedIn is the fastest-growing online network, with more than 8.5 million professionals from around the world representing 130 industries.[71]

When you join, you create a profile that summarizes your professional accomplishments. Your profile helps you find and be found by former colleagues, clients, and partners. You can add more connections by inviting trusted contacts to join LinkedIn and connect to you. Your network consists of your connections and your connections' connections, linking you to thousands of qualified professionals.

This network is great for business development and for those looking for a new job. But in addition, when you create your profile, you describe your interests and groups affiliations. Therefore, you can search for people with the same interests or see to which other groups people with profiles similar to yours belong and get information on those groups for professional or social purposes. You can search by any criteria from industry to geographical location, university attended, etc.

And here is a great example of how LinkedIn works. My former classmate, whom I haven't seen for years, found me through this system, and now we are in touch again.

**This Guide's Blog**

*http://legalaliensguide.blogspot.com*

My aim is to make my *Guide* a dynamic, not static, document. While the printed *Guide* is the core, the blog will be a living document where I will regularly post additions to the book. Updates will include new organizations and clubs, interesting upcoming networking events, and personal stories and advice. This way, my book will never be out-of-date and will always be relevant to you.

---

71    The information is from LinkedIn Web site

# CHAPTER 14:
# HOW TO MAKE THE
# MOST OF IT

This guide provides you with more than a hundred links to various organizations and resources; however, the question remains: how can you get the most benefit from them?

Based on my own experience, I can advise you the following:

1. **Define your goal.** Do you want to find a job, to start your own business, or just to socialize and find friends? After defining you goal, you can study the relevant chapter in this book.

2. **Focus.** You won't be able to devote your time to all the organizations and clubs in a selected category. But it makes sense to check out most of them once to form your own opinion. Remember, most of the organizations will allow you to attend one or two events for free before becoming a member.

3. **Make your choice.** If resources (time and budget) are limited, I recommend that you choose the three following networks or groups:

   - Join a **local and/or national group.** Your local group may be your community church or local chamber of commerce. Churches will have free job-support groups and loads information on local community events. A chamber of commerce will help you with business-related issues, and, in addition, chambers of commerce very often organize social events for the whole family. As an example, Lakeview East CC of Chicago organizes great family events for Halloween and Christmas.

If you are coming to the United States from abroad, definitely get in touch with your country's chamber of commerce. This is your "home away from home." You will be able to meet your compatriots, attend cultural events, etc.

Personally, I joined a local church community, my local chamber of commerce, and the French American Chamber of Commerce. You are probably wondering why FACC. Well, Chicago does not have a Russian American chamber of commerce, but I love France, I speak French, and the events that FACC organizes are always great.

- Join your **professional group**. This is a must because it's the best place for professional development, business networking, learning more about your profession and industry in the United States, looking for a job, and meeting likeminded people who share your interests.

I joined the Institute of Management Consultants USA when I came to America, and I attended several events organized by the American Marketing Association because my background is in marketing, consulting, and international business.

- Join a **minority** group. If you are an ethnic minority or a woman in the United States, there are plenty of support groups for all purposes that will promote your interests and help you in all sorts of ways from making social connections to starting up your business.

There are many fantastic organizations for women in America. I joined the National Association of Women Business Owners. NAWBO helps me with my business development, and I have made a lot of friends there.

To get full benefits from your membership in any organization, don't just join—**become involved**! Join committees, panels, boards, roundtables, etc. These are smaller groups, and joining them is free once you became a member of the organization. In this way, you will get to know a smaller group of people more intimately; this is the ideal way to start building true connections that will help you to find a job or develop your own business—whatever you need. In addition, you will be able to address issues that are of interest and importance to you. When I joined NAWBO, I immediately became a member of the Diversity committee and the Under-35 roundtable because the issues of diversity at work and the problems that young professionals face are very relevant to me.

If you are interested in a certain networking organization but there is no chapter or subgroup in your city or state you can start one in your location. Many of the organizations I described in this guide support such initiative.

If your goal is specifically business development, then you should think about joining leads groups and a speakers' bureau. The latter will increase your visibility and will serve as a virtually free marketing tool to promote yourself and your business. Many organizations (including some chambers of commerce, professional organizations, National Association of Women Business Owners, etc.) will have speaking opportunities.

There is also an independent free speakers' bureau resource in Chicago called **Free Speech.** Its Web address is *http://www.gr-pr.com/freespeech.html.*

I also strongly advise you to use this time in transition for **personal and professional development.** When you settle down, find a job, or start your own business, you won't have time for educational opportunities, so use the time you have on hand now. A lot of organizations hold various seminars and workshops for a minimal fee or for free. Consider learning a language or attending some professional seminars.

I love events that are organized in my professional area by Northwestern University, the American Marketing Association, and the Institute of Management Consultants. I always try to find time to attend the most interesting events. Don't forget that these events are not only good for educational purposes but good for networking as well.

# CHAPTER 15: CONCLUSION

I sincerely hope that the information in this book is helpful to you. I suffered in ignorance so that you don't have to. I tried to make my *Guide* useful for everyone coming to Chicago and for Americans who wish to start their life anew.

I tried to make this book current, and I will do my best to keep it this way for years to come. Because life never stops, things develop, and new organizations emerge, **this book is accompanied by a blog** *http://legalaliensguide.blogspot.com* at which I will regularly post updates for the book, listing new networks, interesting upcoming events and opportunities, and more.

I hope you found my book enjoyable, and if you have any questions or comments, you are welcome to post them on the blog. I cannot guarantee that I will be able to respond to all of them, but I will try to do my best.

Good luck to you in your new journey!

# APPENDIX 1:
# JOB CLUBS IN ILLINOIS[72]

| Town | Networking Group Info |
|------|----------------------|
| RADIO | Job Talk Radio<br>WJJG AM 1530<br>Weekly broadcast LIVE Thursdays from 4:00 to 5:00 PM; taped Monday 9:00 to 10:00 AM<br>Live call in phone number: 708-493-1530<br>Live radio talk show to help listeners find a job, start a business, or change careers<br>homepage.mac.com/mikebaker/WJJG.html<br>Contact: Terry Tierney<br>Phone: 847-989-2503<br>E-mail: jobtalkusa@yahoo.com |
| ARLINGTON HEIGHTS | Arlington Heights One-Stop Career Center<br>IETC, BEST TEAM<br>723 Algonquin Road<br>Arlington Heights, IL 60005<br>Contact: Ted Kasch<br>Direct Phone: 847-437-8913<br>Or Office Phone: 847-981-7400 ext. 78913<br>Fax: 847-981-7182<br>E-mail: tedk@arlingtonheights.ietcnetwork.org<br>Web site: http://arlingtonheights.ietcnetwork.org |

---

72 This information is diligently put together and graciously provided by Pat Harrington from Business Network Chicago.

| Town | Networking Group Info |
|------|----------------------|
| ARLINGTON HEIGHTS | Business Employer Service Team<br>723 Algonquin Road<br>Arlington Heights, IL 60005<br>Contact: Ted Kasch<br>Direct Phone: 847-437-8913<br>Or Office Phone: 847-981-7400 ext. 78913<br>Fax: 847-981-7182<br>E-mail: tkasch@worknetncc.com<br>Networking Meeting 2nd and 4th Wednesday of each month at 2:00 PM |
| BARRINGTON | Barrington Career Center (BCC)<br>600 Hart Road Suite 275<br>Barrington, IL 60010<br>Contact: Brian J. Mulcrone, director, or Kathleen Reese, admin. director<br>Phone: 847-304-4157<br>Fax: 847-304-4163<br>E-mail: bccenter@ameritech.net<br>Web site: bakhome.northstarnet.org/bccenter/<br>1. Two networking meetings are scheduled every Tuesday morning, 7:30 to 9:30 AM and 10:00 AM to noon.<br>2. Job-skill-building seminars are held Thursday evenings from 7:00 to 9:00 PM.<br>3. "Lean Mean Interviewing Skills" workshop on 1st and 3rd Wednesday afternoons from 12:00 to 4:00 PM (an interactive workshop dealing with job-interview role playing)<br>4. Job-search advisors offer guidance by appointment throughout the week during office hours and on Monday evenings from 6:00 to 9:00 PM. |
| BARRINGTON | Career Transitions Workshop & LifeWork Workshops<br>Willow Creek Community Church<br>67 E. Algonquin road<br>S. Barrington, IL 60010<br>Phone: 224-512-1892 |

| Town | Networking Group Info |
|------|----------------------|
| | E-mail: <u>careers@willowcreek.org</u><br>Web site: http://www.willowcreek.org/careers.asp<br>Workshops meet Monday nights from 7 to 9 PM; both workshops run for six weeks. |
| BARTLETT | Career Transitioners Networking Group<br>Living Lord Lutheran Church<br>1044 Congress Drive<br>Bartlett, IL 60103<br>Contact: Pastor Steve Meyers<br>Phone: 630-830-3630 ext. 4608<br>E-mail: CTersEB@yahoogroups.com<br>Meets every Tuesday evening from 7:00 to 8:30 PM |
| BENSENVILLE | Job Search Club<br>Bensenville Community Public Library<br>200 S. Church Rd.<br>Bensenville, IL 60106<br>Contact: Judy McGah<br>Phone: 630-495-4345 ext. 232<br>Meets once a week., |
| CHICAGO | Able Career Institute™ (ACI) of National Able Network, Inc.<br>A training and education institution that focuses on enhancing skills for the workforce. The institute offers a variety of classes and training opportunities to enable career advancement. ACI is offering free basic computer-training classes to people who are interested in expanding their computer knowledge to meet workforce demands.<br>Contact: Melinda Crosby, director of career services<br>Phone: 312-580-1498.<br>National Able Network<br>180 N. Wabash Suite 600<br>Chicago, IL 60611<br>Web site: http://www.nationalable.org |

| Town | Networking Group Info |
| --- | --- |
| CHICAGO | ITA—Illinois Technology Association & Fastroot Technology Inc.<br>Illinois IT Association (ITA)<br>200 S. Wacker—15th Floor<br>Chicago, IL 60606<br>Contact: Sarah Habansky, manager, programs and events<br>Phone: 312-924-1077<br>E-mail: shabansky@illinoistech.org<br>Web site: headquarters@illinoistech.org<br>ITA and Fastroot Technology, Inc. invite you to join friends, colleagues, and competitors in the local technology community to take time away from the daily workload to bring together Illinois's technology executives to mingle and collaborate. |
| CHICAGO | Marketing and Mar/Com Group meeting<br>DBM conference room<br>55 W. Monroe, 29th floor<br>Chicago, IL<br>Contact: Neal Sosnowski, Hoyne Associates, Inc.<br>E-mail: Neal@HoyneAssociates.com<br>Phone: 773-227-3813<br>Fax: 773-772-7661<br>Marketing and marketing communication professionals in transition Group meets every two weeks on Fridays from 10:00 to 11:30 AM<br>Subscribe to Yahoo! group: dbmgroup-subscribe@yahoogroups.com |
| DOWNERS GROVE | Ops/Supply Chain Networking Group<br>DBM (Drake Beam Morin Offices)<br>4th Floor—Suite 400<br>1901 Butterfield Rd<br>Downers Grove, IL 60515<br>Dates: 1st and 3rd Tuesdays of the month from 10 AM to noon |

| Town | Networking Group Info |
|------|----------------------|
| | Contact: David Otto<br>Phone: 630-212-6635 (cell)<br>E-mail: DOtto45321@aol.com |
| ELGIN | Elgin Job Club<br>Elgin Illinois Employment & Training Center<br>30 DuPage Court<br>Elgin, IL 60120<br>Contact: Jen Duchaj<br>Phone: 847-888-7900 ext. 247<br>Meetings are held on Fridays from 9 to 10:30 AM. To participate, contact Kathy Wall, KCDEE, Elgin IETC at 847-888-7900 ext. 293. Job Club is an informative and interactive session guided by professionals from Elgin Community College (ECC), Illinois Department of Employment Security (IDES), and Kane County Department of Employment and Education (KCDEE). |
| ELMHURST | Executive Resources Center<br>124 N. York Road, Suite 280<br>Elmhurst, IL 60126-2811<br>Contact: Tom Horn, executive director<br>Phone: 630-546-9430<br>E-mail: thorne@executiveresources.org<br>Web site: http://www.executiveresources.org |
| GLEN ELLYN | Career Vision<br>800 Roosevelt Road, Suite E-200<br>Glen Ellyn, IL 60137-5866<br>Phone: 800 469-8378<br>E-mail: info@careervision.org<br>Web Site: http://www.careervision.org/ |
| GLEN ELLYN | DuPage Executive Network (The DEN)<br>College of DuPage<br>425 Fawell<br>Glen Ellyn, IL 60137<br>Building K-305, Parking Lot 10 |

| Town | Networking Group Info |
|------|----------------------|
|  | Door K-2, West Commons<br>Phone: 630-942-2230<br>E-mail: den@cdnet.cod.edu<br>Web site: http://www.cod-theden.com<br>Meets every fourth Tuesday of the month from 9:00 AM to 2:00 PM<br>Group for senior management executives working in career transition with minimum base of $75,000 in last position |
| LAKE FOREST | Career Resource Center<br>Lake Forest Symphony Music School<br>40 East Old Mill Road, Suite 105<br>Lake Forest, IL 60045<br>Contact: Jan Cline Leahy, Director<br>Phone: 847-295-5626<br>Fax: 847-295-5430<br>E-mail: info@careerresourcecenter.org<br>Web site: http://careerresourcecenter.org/<br>Open Monday, Wednesday, Thursday, and Friday 9:30 AM to 4:30 PM and Tuesday 4:00 PM to 9:00 PM. The processing fee is $40 for all clients.<br>Networking meetings held several Tuesday evenings each month Please check calendar on CRC Web page for specific dates and times. |
| LAKE ZURICH | St. Francis de Sales Ministry Center<br>135 S. Buesching<br>Lake Zurich, IL<br>Contact: 847-438-6622 for more information |
| LISLE/<br>NAPERVILLE | Lisle Township/Family Services Office<br>4721 Indiana Ave.<br>Lisle, IL 60532<br>Phone: 630-469-2771<br>Contact: Steve Gawron or Joy Maguire-Dooley at 630-968-1880 ext. 13 or Al Larson at 847-559-6346 (work) or 630-904-4156 (home) |

| Town | Networking Group Info |
|------|----------------------|
|  | E-mail: executivestatusnetwork@yahoogroups.com<br>Web site: www.lisletownship.com/jobclubs.htm<br>Fee: $2.00 per meeting<br>This networking group is for management level<br>($70,000) and above. Meetings are held the first<br>Monday evening of each month from 7 to 9 PM. |
| LISLE | Lisle Township Job Club<br>Lisle Library<br>777 Front Street<br>Lisle, IL 60532<br>Phone: 630-971-1675<br>Contact: Joy Dooley at 630-968-1880 ext. 49<br>Meets Friday from 10:00 AM to noon<br>Web site: home.xnet.com/~nomads |
| LOMBARD | Illinois Employment Training Center Job Club<br>Eastgate Shopping Center<br>837 South Westmore Avenue<br>Lombard, IL 60148<br>Contact: Jim Fergle<br>Phone: 630-495-4345 ext. 200<br>Meets every Friday morning from 9:30 to noon<br>Guest speakers on career management topics |
| LOMBARD | MFG (Manufacturing Fellowship Group)<br>A manufacturing and manufacturingrelated<br>networking subgroup of the Lisle/Naperville Job Club<br>Helen Plum Memorial Library<br>110 West Maple Street<br>Lombard, IL 60148<br>RSVP to: Juan Chapa, facilitator<br>Phone: 630-272-8023<br>E-mail: Mfgpros@att.net |

| Town | Networking Group Info |
|------|----------------------|
|  | In the lower level auditorium or the second-floor training room. Will be meeting the last Tuesday of each month 6:30 to 8:45 PM. The group is composed of manufacturing and manufacturing-related persons (manufacturing management, QA, HR, material control, procurement, supply chain, distribution, warehousing, industrial & manufacturing engineering, production planning, facilities managers) |
| NAPERVILLE | Chicago Training Network<br>Panera Bread<br>Ogden Avenue & Naperville Road<br>Naperville, IL<br>Contact: Steve Gawron<br>Phone: 630-469-2771<br>E-mail: gawron@megsinet.net<br>Informal monthly networking meeting open and free-of-charge to any person involved in the training industry. You can request membership in our Yahoo! Group by contacting Steve at gawron@megsinet.net. |
| NAPERVILLE | Community Career Center Job Club<br>AMCORE Bank Building, Second Floor<br>1971 Gowdey Road (& Route 59)<br>Naperville, IL 60540<br>Phone: 630-961-5665<br>Fax: 630-961-1271<br>E-mail: info@communitycareercenter.org<br>Web site: www.communitycareercenter.org<br>Contact: Margaret Jensen, executive director<br>Monday, Tuesday, Friday, and Saturday from 10:00 AM to 2:00 PM Wednesday and Thursday from 10:00 AM to 7:00 PM<br>The job club meets every Wednesday from 10:00 AM to 1:00 PM |

| Town | Networking Group Info |
|------|----------------------|
| NAPERVILLE | Training Network-Midwest<br>Business Education Professionals Job Club<br>(instructors, educators, technical writers, e-learning, organizational development, training management)<br>Elitgen Offices, 1300 Iroquois Avenue, Suite 115<br>Naperville, IL 60563<br>Contact: Bryan Thalhammer<br>Phone: 630-469-2771<br>Meetings are held on the 2nd and 4th Tuesdays from 9:00 to 11:30 AM. |
| NORTHBROOK | ITKN—Information Technology Knowledge Network<br>Mission Hills Country Club<br>1700 Mission Hills Drive<br>Northbrook, IL 60062<br>E-mail: dickhughey@comcast.net<br>Web site: www.grayhairmanagement.com<br>Contact: Dick Hughey<br>The iTKN networking group (400+ IT professionals) distributes job opportunities via e-mail to the membership. |
| OAK FOREST | Self Help Jobs Program<br>5825 West 151st Street<br>Oak Forest, IL 60452<br>Contact: Laura Vande Werken<br>Phone: 708-535-6816<br>Meets on Tuesday and Thursday 8:45 AM to 2:45 PM |
| SCHAUMBURG | Technical Sales & Support Professionals Networking Group<br>Dominick's Finer Foods cafeteria<br>1293 E. Higgins Road<br>Schaumburg, IL 60173<br>Contact: Wayne Van Dyne at wvandyne@earthlink.net<br>William Gallagher at wegalla@comcast.net<br>Perry Weinberg at phweinberg@gmail.com |

| Town | Networking Group Info |
|------|----------------------|
|  | Pat Mondy at patrickmondy@comcast.net<br>Don Oehlert at oehlert.don@mindspring.com<br>This event repeats on the first Monday of every month<br>7:00 to 9:00 PM.<br>TSSP Networking was established to provide a networking group of like-minded, talented professionals. The mission of TSSP Networking is to provide a specialized career-networking group dedicated to the needs of IT sales and sales-support professionals, IT managers, and project managers. |
| SKOKIE | FREE Career Counselor<br>Skokie Public Library<br>5215 Oakton Street<br>Skokie, IL 60077<br>Contact: Phyllis Cable from JVS<br>Phone: 847-673-7774 ext. 2127<br>Third Tuesday of each month. Call to schedule an appointment. |
| SKOKIE | Job and Career Support Group<br>Skokie Public Library<br>5215 Oakton Street<br>Skokie, IL 60077<br>Contact: Mike Buhmann<br>E-mail: buhmm@skokie.lib.il.us<br>Phone: 847-673-3762 ext. 4126<br>Web site: www.chicagojobs.org<br>Meets each 3rd Monday of the month 9:30 to 11:00 AM |
| SOUTH HOLLAND | Self Help Jobs Program<br>Peace CRC<br>833 East 168th Street<br>South Holland, IL 60473<br>Contact: Linda Lester, director<br>Phone: 708-596-2887<br>Tuesday and Thursday 10:00 AM to 4:00 PM |

| Town | Networking Group Info |
|------|------------------------|
| ST. CHARLES, GENEVA, BATAVIA | Tri-Cities Unemployment Group (TUG)<br>1 South 6th Avenue<br>St. Charles, IL 60174<br>Contact: Heidi Johnson<br>Phone: 630-631-1871<br>E-mail: info@tricityug.org.<br>Web site: www.tricityug.org<br>Meetings are held every other Monday evening from 6:30 to 9:00 PM at the St. Charles Public Library. Following the speaker presentations, breakout groups will be formed to share backgrounds and practice the elevator speech. Please bring resumes, handbills or business cards, leads, and company contacts if you are interested in networking. |
| SUGAR GROVE | Career Vision Book Review Series<br>Sugar Grove Public Library<br>54 Snow Street<br>Sugar Grove, IL 60554<br>Contact: Christy Seawall, certified career coach and counselor, Career Vision Dynamics<br>Phone: 630-466-4686<br>Web site: www.careervisiondynamics.com<br>Meetings are held every 4th Thursday at the library from 7 to 8 PM. |
| WOODRIDGE | Resume Critiques<br>Woodridge Public Library<br>3 Plaza Drive<br>Woodridge, IL 60517<br>Contact: Susan Peterson<br>Phone: 630-968-1880 ext. 232<br>Web site: www.woodridgelibrary.org/calendar/allevents_current.html<br>Resume writing session every Monday from 10:00 AM to noon |

| Town | Networking Group Info |
|------|----------------------|
| WOODSTOCK | Network to Success<br>McHenry County Job Training<br>400 Russell Ct.<br>Woodstock, IL 60098-2614<br>Phone: 815-338-7100 ext. 228<br>Fax: 815-338-7125<br>Contact: Mary Stoerp, training/career counselor, to reserve space<br>Meetings are held every 2nd and 4th Wednesday from 1 to 4 PM. |

# APPENDIX 2:
## USEFUL SERVICES

In this chapter, I would like to draw my readers' attention to a number of specific organizations—such as financial and real-estate institutions—whose services do not include networking but are nonetheless essential for any newcomer. They will help you to rebuild your life in a new place. I decided to recommend these organizations and people because I know them personally either through our joint work in NAWBO (National Association of Women Business Owners) or through being their customer myself (for example, we use WDT at home)

## TELECOMMUNICATIONS

**World Discount Telecommunications, Inc.**
WDT is a long-distance service that allows you to call your friends and relatives abroad from your home or cell phone at very competitive rates. No need to buy calling cards anymore! They offer you affordable prices, reliable connection, and excellent multilingual customer service.

World Discount Telecommunications, Inc.
Phone: 1-888-6060-938
www.mywdt.com

## TAX/AUDIT/CONSULTING SERVICES

**Blackman Kallick**
Blackman Kallick is among the ten largest accounting and consulting firms in Chicago. They provide audit, tax, and consulting services for privately held and publicly traded companies, not-for-profit organizations, and high-net-worth

families and individuals. They are proud of their reputation as a firm of uncompromising integrity that delivers exceptional client service

Blackman Kallick
10 South Riverside Plaza, 9th Floor
Chicago, IL 60606
Contact: Amber Larsen
Direct: 312-980-2964
Main: 312-207-1040
E-mail: alarsen@BlackmanKallick.com
www.BlackmanKallick.com

# FINANCIAL ADVICE

### Michele Conti & Jessica Merino, Ameriprise Financial Services
Michele Conti and Jessica Merino are personal advisors with Ameriprise Financial Services. They are experienced in the financial planning arena and have a strong passion for helping others. Their comprehensive practices focus on helping clients accumulate tax-free wealth and lean about investment strategies, education planning, retirement planning, insurance, and estate planning.

Michele L. Conti
Financial Advisor
Ameriprise Financial Services, Inc.
8700 West Bryn Mawr Avenue, Suite 1000 North
Chicago, IL 60631
Office: 773-628-2229
E-mail: Michele.L.Conti@ampf.com

Jessica L. Merino
Ameriprise Financial Services, Inc.
One Northbrook Place-5 Revere Drive, Suite 200
Northbrook, IL 60062
Office: 847-498-7390
E-mail: Jessica.L.Merino@ampf.com

# REAL ESTATE SERVICES

**Diane Diedrich, Coldwell Banker**
Diane is a real-estate veteran with over fifteen years of experience. Diane's success is attributed to her knowledge of the market and her professionalism, persistence, and overall service and caring to her clients. Her services include helping buyers and sellers with all of their real-estate needs in Chicago; however, she can refer to anywhere in the United States.

Diane Diedrich
Coldwell Banker
1959 North Halstead
Chicago, IL 60614
Phone: 312-867-8309
Fax: 312-943-9779
E-mail: diane.diedrich@cbexchange.com
www.dianediedrich.com

# MORTGAGE BROKER

**Perl Mortgage/AAA Commercial Mortgage Group**
Perl Mortgage and AAA-CMG are always looking to better serve their clients. They differentiate themselves by offering a superior level of service in addition to aggressive rates. They strive to develop a long-term relationship with clients, requiring them to pay very close attention to satisfying personal financial needs. Pearl Mortgage will be very glad to become your "your lender for life".

Eric Medina, Perl Mortgage/AAA Commercial Mortgage Group
2936 W. Belmont Avenue Chicago, IL 60618
Phone: 773-413-6202, mobile: 847-207-5400
E-mail: eric.medina@perlmortgage.com
www.perlmortgage.com, www.AAA-CMG.com

# LEGAL SERVICES

**Scott D. Pollock & Associates, P.C.**
Scott D. Pollock & Associates, P.C. has received a rating of "AV" (very high to preeminent) from Martindale-Hubbel. The firm provides legal representation

in the area of immigration and nationality law to businesses and individuals in the United States and abroad. They are available for consultation and representation on a wide variety of immigration matters including family and employment-based immigration, immigrant and nonimmigrant visa processing, requirements for employment authorization, employer sanctions, political asylum, and deportation/exclusion matters.

Kathryn R. Weber, Attorney
Scott D. Pollock & Associates, P.C.
105 W. Madison Street, Suite 2200
Chicago, IL 60602
Phone: 312-444-1940
Fax: 312-444-1950
E-mail:kweber@lawfirm1.com
www.lawfirm1.com

# EDUCATIONAL SERVICES

**Application 2 Graduation**
Application 2 Graduation successfully manages the process of U.S. college selection, application, financial aid, internship, and graduation. They provide four years of personalized support to ensure that their clients obtain a quality college education that promotes academic and social growth. They help you to piece together the college dream.

Application 2 Graduation, LLC
225 West Washington Street, Suite 2200
Chicago, Illinois 60606
Phone: 773-934-8910
E-mail: info@application2graduation.com
www.application2graduation.com

# NOTES

# NOTES

# NOTES

978-0-595-44622-3
0-595-44622-1